Table of Contents

From Field to Faith

**Linking Jewish Agricultural Feasts with Catholic Sacraments
of Initiation**

by

Dr. ant

endorses the information the organization or website may provide or recommendations it may make.

Please remember that Internet websites listed in this work may have changed or disappeared between when this work was written and when it is read.

Contents

Introduction: Understanding the Journey from Judaism to Catholicism

At the heart of every deep-seated faith transition lies a journey—a path strewn with historical, spiritual, and personal transitions that draw the sojourner ever closer to the Truth. The passage from Judaism to Catholicism is one of profound significance, embodying a transition that is both a fulfillment and a beginning. It is a journey that invites exploration into the rich tapestry of faith that connects the Old and the New, the Promised and the Fulfilled.

The fabric of this journey is woven with threads of ancient traditions, sacred scriptures, and the profound understanding that Catholicism stands not in opposition but in glorious continuation of Judaism. This understanding is pivotal, especially in a world where the lines of religious and spiritual identity are often drawn with sharp, divisive edges. By tracing the lineage of faith from Judaism through to Catholicism, one uncovers a narrative of divine revelation and fulfillment that is both enlightening and transformative.

This transition is underpinned by the sacred texts that form the bedrock of both faiths. The Hebrew Scriptures, revered within Judaism, serve as a precursor to the New Testament of the Catholic Church, with the latter fulfilling the prophecies and promises found within the former. The essence of Catholicism is deeply rooted in Judaism, a fact that becomes increasingly evident as one delves into the theological, liturgical, and spiritual continuities between the two.

The sacramentality of Catholicism, with its profound emphasis on visible signs of invisible grace, finds its antecedents in the rich symbolism and ritual of Jewish law and tradition. From the agricultural feasts of the Jewish calendar to the sacraments of initiation within the Catholic Church, there exists a thematic and spiritual connection that binds the two in a continuity of faith. This connection is a testament to the enduring promise of salvation that flows through the history of the chosen people, from Abraham to the apostles, and into the heart of the Church today.

Understanding this journey requires an exploration of both the historical roots and the unfolding present. The agricultural feasts of Judaism—Passover, Pentecost, and Tabernacles—find their fulfillment in the sacraments of initiation in Catholicism— Baptism, Confirmation, and the Eucharist. Each step of this transition is laden with theological significance, revealing the ways in which the sacraments serve as the ultimate culmination of Jewish faith and tradition.

The narrative arc from Barley to Wheat to Grapes, symbolizing progression from Judaism to Catholicism, encapsulates a spiritual evolution that is both individual and collective. This evolution is not merely a change of religious affiliation but a deepened engagement with the divine mystery that stands at the heart of human existence.

Addressing the theological underpinnings of this journey demands a discourse that is both persuasive and deeply informed by sacred scripture. It invites an examination of how Catholic sacraments act as the fulfillment of scriptural prophecy, embodying the means through which believers are drawn into a closer communion with the Divine. In this light, Catholicism is seen not as a replacement but as the natural progression of the covenant established with the people of Israel.

For those who embark on this journey, the path from Judaism to Catholicism is marked by challenges and questions. Engaging with these challenges requires a compassionate and reasoned discourse that respects the profundity of Jewish faith while illuminating the truth of Catholicism as the fulfillment of God's promises.

Conversion, therefore, is understood not merely as a change in religious practice but as a heartfelt response to the call of God—a call that beckons across the ages, inviting all into the fullness of truth and salvation. The Catholic Church, in reaching out to Jewish believers, does so with the deep conviction that within her lies the promise of unity and the fulfillment of the law and the prophets.

This journey of faith is, at its core, a pilgrimage toward truth and unity. It is a path that leads from the particular to the universal, from the promised to the fulfilled. It is a testament to the enduring love of God, who guides His people through the ages toward the fullness of redemption.

Therefore, this introduction sets the stage for a thorough exploration of the themes, traditions, and theological insights that illuminate the path from Judaism to Catholicism. It is an invitation to readers—Catholics, biblical scholars, university professors, students, and Jewish converts to Catholicism—to engage deeply with the profound continuity of faith that binds the Church to her roots in Israel.

The goal of this book is to exalt and propagate the Holy Roman Catholic Church, to invite conversion among the Jewish faithful, and to establish Catholicism as the fulfillment of Judaism and the means of salvation. In doing so, it seeks to engage readers in a persuasive, scientifically rigorous, and biblically rich discourse that honors the journey of faith that links these two great traditions.

The journey from Judaism to Catholicism is a testament to the power of divine revelation and the persistence of faith. It invites an exploration that is both historical and contemporary, personal and communal. It is a path strewn with challenges, but also with the light of understanding, beckoning all toward the fullness of truth.

Thus, as we delve into the chapters that follow, let us keep in mind the profound connections and the sacred journey that invite Jews and Catholics alike into a deeper understanding of faith, fulfillment, and salvation. Let this book serve as a guide, a companion, and a source of inspiration for all who embark on this spiritual journey.

References:

The Historical Roots of Jewish Agricultural Feasts

In the sacred narrative of history, the Jewish agricultural feasts stand as pivotal markers, encapsulating the spiritual richness and providential care bestowed upon the Israelites. Among these, Passover, Pentecost, and Tabernacles emerge not merely as celebrations of temporal bounty but as profound symbols foretelling the fulfillment of divine promises through Catholicism. This chapter delves into the historical and agricultural underpinnings of these feasts, setting the stage for a deeper appreciation of their spiritual significance and their role in illuminating the path from Judaism to the Holy Roman Catholic Church.

Passover, the first of these feasts, commemorates the Israelites' deliverance from Egyptian bondage, anchored in the agricultural cycle through the harvest of barley. This period of liberation and gratitude is paralleled in Catholicism through the sacrament of Baptism, which signifies the believer's passage from the slavery of sin to the freedom of the children of God (Hahn, 2009). Just as the first fruits of barley were offered in thanksgiving, so too is the soul cleansed in Baptism, presented as a first fruit of the New Covenant promised by Christ.

Following Passover is Pentecost, celebrating the wheat harvest, fifty days later. In Jewish tradition, it also commemorates the giving of the Torah on Mount Sinai, a time of receiving divine instruction. For Catholics, this feast finds its fulfillment in the sacrament of Confirmation, where believers are imbued with the Holy Spirit, equipped and strengthened to live out the commandments of God's law in the newness of spirit, not in the oldness of the letter (Scott, 1997). This parallel underscores the transformation of the Law through the outpouring of the Spirit, leading to a harvest of righteousness.

The Feast of Tabernacles, celebrated at the culmination of the agricultural year with the grape harvest, invites the faithful to dwell in temporary shelters, recalling Israel's sojourn in the wilderness. This celebration prefigures the Eucharist, where Catholics partake of the true vine, Jesus Christ (Bruce, 2014). The Eucharist is the source and summit of Christian life, the ultimate thanksgiving and consummation of God's plan of salvation, offering the faithful a foretaste of the heavenly banquet.

Through this exploration, it becomes evident that the agricultural roots of these Jewish feasts were divinely instituted not merely for temporal sustenance but as a shadow of the things to come in the fullness of time through the Catholic Church. As such, understanding their historical and spiritual dimensions reveals the deep connections between Judaism and Catholicism, with the latter fulfilling and transcending the former in the plan of divine salvation. The journey from barley to wheat to grapes in these festivals mirrors the spiritual journey of humanity from bondage to liberation, from law to grace, and from sojourning to eternal dwelling with God.

Understanding Passover, Pentecost, and Tabernacles

The exploration of the historical roots of Jewish agricultural feasts invites an understanding that transcends mere ritual observance, revealing a profound theological tapestry interwoven with the promises of salvation history. It is within this context that the feasts of Passover, Pentecost, and Tabernacles emerge not only as commemorations of God's past actions but as eschatological signposts pointing towards the fulfillment of divine promises in the Catholic Church. Passover, Pentecost, and Tabernacles are intertwined with the Jewish agricultural calendar, embodying the seamless blend of physical sustenance and spiritual nourishment.

Passover, or Pesach in Hebrew, commemorates the Exodus from Egypt, when the Israelites were freed from bondage. This feast is deeply agricultural, closely tied to the barley harvest. It marks a beginning, a divine intervention in history to liberate a chosen people. Yet, the Passover's lamb, whose blood marked the houses of the Israelites, prefigures Christ, the Lamb of God, whose sacrifice on the Cross marks the new covenant and offers liberation from the bondage of sin (Exodus 12:1-14). In this pivotal event, one can see the embryonic promise of baptism, where one is cleansed and reborn.

Pentecost, or Shavuot, occurs fifty days after Passover and commemorates the giving of the Torah at Mount Sinai, as well as celebrating the wheat harvest. This feast is characterized by the offering of the first fruits, emblematic of Israel's gratitude and acknowledgment of God's provision. The Pentecostal event in the Acts of the Apostles, where the Holy Spirit descended upon the apostles, fulfills this feast in a new and profound way, transforming it from a celebration of the Law to a celebration of the Spirit's empowering presence, guiding the Church into all truth (Acts 2).

Tabernacles, or Sukkot, is celebrated in the fall and recalls the forty years of wandering in the desert, living in temporary shelters. It is closely associated with the grape harvest and is a time of joyous celebration, reflecting God's provision and protection. The Gospel of John depicts Jesus attending the feast of Tabernacles and speaking of living water, symbolizing the outpouring of the Holy Spirit (John 7:37-39). This imagery beautifully captures the feast's fulfillment in Christ, who is the true vine (John 15:1), and the Eucharist, which is the source and summit of Christian life.

The Passover lamb, the Pentecostal giving of the Law, and the celebratory nature of Tabernacles find their consummation in the person of Christ and the establishment of the New Covenant in His blood. Each feast, rich in agricultural symbolism, transcends its initial purpose to point towards the mysteries of the Catholic faith. The barley of Passover, the wheat of Pentecost, and the grapes of Tabernacles are not merely physical sustenance but signify the spiritual nurturance provided through the sacraments of Baptism, Confirmation, and the Eucharist respectively.

It is within the Paschal mystery that the Christian finds the true Passover, where Christ's sacrifice becomes the means of liberation from sin and death. Pentecost in the Catholic understanding transforms from a celebration of the Law's reception to an outpouring of the Spirit, enabling the faithful to live out the demands of the Gospel. Lastly, the Feast of Tabernacles calls believers to rejoice in God's sheltering presence, fully realized in the Eucharist, where the faithful partake of the true body and blood of Christ.

In contemplating these feasts, one appreciates their evolutive trajectory from Jewish agricultural festivals to cornerstones of Christian salvation history. They serve as bridges, connecting the Old Covenant with the New, demonstrating the Catholic faith as the true successor of Judaism. In this light, the shift from observing these feasts in their Jewish context to understanding their fulfillment in Catholic sacramentality isn't one of replacement but of completion.

Furthermore, the Catholic Church's liturgical year, with its seasons and feasts, mirrors the agricultural rhythm of planting and harvest, death and rebirth. This rhythm, evident in the Jewish feasts, continues to inform the Catholic understanding of time as sacramental, where earthly cycles reflect heavenly realities. Thus, the Church's liturgical observances are not merely commemorative but are participatory, enabling the faithful to enter into the mysteries they celebrate.

Therefore, the historical roots of these Jewish feasts illuminate the Catholic Church's claim to be the fulfillment of God's salvific plan. Through the Paschal Mystery, Pentecost, and the celebration of the Eucharist, what was shadow in the Old Covenant finds its substance in the New. This theological continuity underscores the Church's mission to gather all peoples into the one family of God, as foretold by the prophets and accomplished in Christ.

The conversion of Jews to Catholicism, then, is seen not as a rejection of their heritage but as its fulfillment. The Catholic faith offers the fullness of revelation, bringing to completion the promises embedded within the Jewish feasts. It is an invitation to enter into a deeper understanding of God's salvific plan, realized in the person of Jesus Christ and lived through the sacraments of the Church.

In conclusion, the feasts of Passover, Pentecost, and Tabernacles serve as historical and theological signposts, guiding the Jewish people through the agricultural year and pointing Christians towards the mysteries of faith. These feasts, once centered on the rhythms of planting and harvest, now celebrate the cycle of redemption accomplished in Christ. As such, they stand as a testament to the Catholic Church's role as the custodian of salvation history, inviting all to partake of the divine mysteries that they foreshadow and fulfill.

Passover and the Harvest of Barley As we reflect on the rich tapestry of feasts that define the Jewish agricultural calendar, we delve into the significance of Passover and its indelible connection to the harvest of barley. This analysis critically examines how this pivotal time not only represents a period of historical and spiritual remembrance for the Jewish people but also serves as a profound metaphor for the Catholic understanding of salvation and transformation.

Passover, or Pesach, commemorates the Israelites' exodus from Egypt, marking their liberation from bondage and their journey towards the Promised Land. This event is not just historical but deeply symbolic, representing freedom from sin and the promise of spiritual salvation. In the context of Catholicism, this liberation is echoed in the sacrament of Baptism, where believers are freed from original sin and begin their journey towards spiritual enlightenment.

The timing of Passover is significantly intertwined with the harvest of barley, the first grain to ripen in the land of Israel. This synchronization is not merely coincidental but imbued with deep symbolic value. Barley's ripening marks the beginning of the harvest season, symbolizing new life, hope, and the promise of sustenance.

Leviticus 23:5-14 details the offering of the barley sheaf, or omer, which is to be presented the day after the Sabbath of Passover week. This act of offering the first fruits of the harvest acknowledges God's providence and blessings – a theme that resonates deeply within Catholic sacramental life, where the Eucharist celebrates Christ as the true Bread of Life, offering Himself for the salvation of the world.

This connection between the physical sustenance provided by the harvest and the spiritual nourishment offered through Christ's sacrifice is central to understanding the fulfillment of Judaism within Catholicism. Just as the barley harvest represented the hope of physical deliverance, so too does the Eucharist represent the hope of spiritual deliverance and eternal life.

Furthermore, the process of preparing the barley parallels the refinement of the soul. Barley had to be reaped, threshed, and winnowed before it could be consumed, symbolizing the purification process that believers undergo through penance and sanctification. This purification is akin to the spiritual refinement that occurs through the sacraments of Reconciliation and the Eucharist in Catholic practice.

In the Book of Ruth, the barley harvest provides the backdrop for Ruth's redemption and marriage to Boaz, symbolizing God's providential care for the faithful. This story can be seen as a metaphor for the Church itself, where Christ, the Bridegroom, redeems and marries the Church, His Bride. The barley harvest thus becomes a sign of the Church's unification with Christ.

Moreover, the counting of the Omer, which begins on the second day of Passover and leads up to the feast of Shavuot or Pentecost, symbolizes the anticipation and preparation of the faithful for the receiving of the Torah and, in a Christian context, for the outpouring of the Holy Spirit. This period of waiting and preparation is mirrored in the Catholic liturgical season between Easter and Pentecost.

The transition from the barley to the wheat harvest, culminating in the celebration of Pentecost, depicts a spiritual maturation. This transition can be paralleled with the Catholic journey of faith from Baptism, where one becomes a new creation in Christ, to Confirmation, where one's faith is strengthened and matured by the Holy Spirit.

In this manner, the barley harvest not only sustains the physical body but also serves as a rich allegory for the sustenance of the soul. Through God's providence, both the physical harvest and the spiritual harvest provide for the needs of the faithful, guiding them on their journey towards salvation.

To draw these parallels between Passover, the barley harvest, and Catholic sacramental theology is to reveal the continuation and fulfillment of the Jewish faith in Catholicism. It underscores the Church's teaching that salvation history, revealed through Scripture and tradition, finds its consummation in Christ and the sacraments instituted for the Church.

In conclusion, the Passover celebration and the accompanying barley harvest are not just historical events or agricultural milestones; they are profound symbols of spiritual liberation, purification, and unification. For Catholics, these symbols are not superseded but fulfilled in the person of Jesus Christ, who offers Himself as the ultimate Passover lamb and the bread of life - the true sustenance for our spiritual journey towards eternal life.

In reflecting on the symbols of Passover and the barley harvest, Catholics are invited to deepen their understanding of their faith and the sacraments, recognizing in them the fulfillment of God's salvific plan initiated with the people of Israel. This recognition is a call to unity and a deeper conversion, encouraging Jewish believers to see in the Catholic faith the continuation of their spiritual journey toward God, with Christ as the ultimate fulfilment of the Passover promise.

In engaging with these rich symbols and their fulfillment in Catholic teachings, both Jews and Catholics are beckoned towards a deeper communion, grounded in the shared roots of their faith and the transformative power of God's saving grace. For in the harvest of barley and the feast of Passover, we find not only the anticipation but the very realization of divine promise and providence.

Pentecost and the Wheat Harvest The festival of Pentecost, or Shavuot in Hebrew, is a multifaceted celebration with significant implications for both Judaism and Catholicism. Its origins lie in the wheat harvest, a pivotal event in the agricultural calendar of ancient Israel. This festival, occurring fifty days after Passover, marks not only the end of the barley harvest but also the beginning of the wheat harvest. In this context, the wheat becomes a symbol of God's continual provision and sustenance to His people.

The connection between Pentecost and the wheat harvest offers a profound reflection on the sustenance provided by God, not only physically through the harvest but also spiritually through His revelations. In Judaism, Shavuot commemorates the giving of the Torah at Mount Sinai, a pivotal moment when God revealed His laws and commandments to the Israelites. This event is mirrored in Catholicism through the celebration of Pentecost, which marks the descent of the Holy Spirit upon the apostles and the birth of the Church. The parallels between these two events emphasize the continuity between Judaism and Catholicism, portraying Catholicism as the fulfillment of the promises made in Jewish scripture.

Across the ages, the wheat harvest has been a time of joy and thanksgiving, attributes that are intrinsic to the celebration of Pentecost in Catholic tradition. The gift of the Holy Spirit, considered the first fruits of the Church, is celebrated with joy and gratitude, much like the wheat harvest was in ancient Israel. The Holy Spirit empowers believers, bestowing upon them gifts that enable them to live out their faith fully. This empowerment echoes the sustenance and nourishment provided by the wheat harvest, which enabled the physical survival and prosperity of the people.

The Pentecost event in the New Testament is imbued with the symbolism of the wheat harvest. When the Holy Spirit descended on the apostles, they began to speak in various tongues, a sign of the universal reach of the Church's mission. This mirrors the universality of God's provision through the wheat harvest, which sustains not just one nation but people across the world. The distribution of the Holy Spirit's gifts among believers mirrors the distribution of the harvested wheat, both essential for life and growth.

The timing of Pentecost, fifty days after Passover, is significant in both the Jewish and Catholic liturgical calendars. It links the liberation from Egypt with the giving of the Torah and the death and resurrection of Jesus with the birth of the Church. This timing highlights a journey from liberation to revelation and covenant, embodied in the transition from barley to wheat. Just as barley is the first crop to ripen, signifying the initial liberation of Passover, wheat matures later, symbolizing the deeper sustenance provided through revelation and the Holy Spirit.

In ancient Israel, the offering of the first fruits of the wheat harvest at Pentecost was a gesture of thanksgiving and dedication to God. This is paralleled in Catholicism by the offering of oneself to God through the invocation of the Holy Spirit. The act of offering the first fruits is a sign of trust and dependence on God, acknowledging that all provision comes from Him. This gesture is perpetuated in the Church's sacrament of Confirmation, where believers offer themselves to God, seeking the seal of the Holy Spirit.

The transition from the physical sustenance provided by the wheat harvest to the spiritual sustenance provided by the Holy Spirit underscores a broader theological theme of progress from the material to the spiritual. This theme resonates deeply with the Catholic understanding of the sacraments as means of grace that sustain and nourish the believer's spiritual life. Just as the wheat sustains the body, the Holy Spirit sustains the soul, guiding, and empowering believers to live according to God's will.

The agricultural cycle of planting, growth, and harvest serves as a metaphor for spiritual growth and maturation in both Judaism and Catholicism. The journey from Passover to Pentecost reflects a spiritual journey from redemption to sanctification, a theme that is central to both faiths. The culmination of this journey at Pentecost, with the giving of the Torah and the descent of the Holy Spirit, represents the fullness of revelation and the empowerment to live out that revelation in everyday life.

The theme of covenant is also central to the celebrations of Pentecost in both Judaism and Catholicism. The giving of the Torah and the descent of the Holy Spirit are both seen as covenantal acts, where God establishes a special relationship with His people. These events are not viewed merely as historical occurrences but as ongoing realities that continue to shape the lives of believers.

In Catholic theology, the notion of harvest extends beyond the physical gathering of crops to include the harvesting of souls for the kingdom of God. The celebration of Pentecost, therefore, has an evangelistic dimension, reflecting the Church's mission to spread the Gospel throughout the world. This mission is sustained by the Holy Spirit, who equips believers with the necessary gifts and fruits to be effective witnesses of Christ's love and salvation.

The imagery of wheat and bread in the context of Pentecost also has Eucharistic connotations in Catholicism. Just as wheat is transformed into bread, which sustains the body, the bread of the Eucharist is transformed into the Body of Christ, which sustains the soul. This transformation reflects the action of the Holy Spirit, who sanctifies and brings to fulfillment God's plan of salvation. The celebration of Pentecost, therefore, is not only a commemoration of a historical event but also a celebration of the ongoing work of the Holy Spirit in the Church and in the lives of believers.

In conclusion, the festival of Pentecost and the wheat harvest encapsulate significant theological themes that resonate across Judaism and Catholicism. The celebration of this festival highlights the continuity between these two faiths, portraying Catholicism as the fulfillment of the promises made in Jewish scripture. Through the lens of Pentecost, we see the journey from physical sustenance to spiritual sustenance, from liberation to revelation and covenant, and from the individual to the universal Church. This festival reminds us of God's continual provision, both physically through the harvest and spiritually through His revelations, encouraging believers to live out their faith empowered by the Holy Spirit.

Tabernacles and the Grape Harvest The Feast of Tabernacles, also known as Sukkot in the Jewish tradition, is a festival that has rich agricultural and theological significance, marking the end of the harvest season and commemorating the protection God provided for the Israelites during their 40 years in the desert after the Exodus from Egypt. This festival is celebrated in the early fall, when the grape harvest is completed. The intertwining of the agricultural and the spiritual in this celebration offers a profound insight into the understanding of God's provisions and protections.

In ancient Israel, the grape harvest was a time of significant joy and festivity, as it marked the culmination of months of toil and the beginning of a period of rest and celebration. The fruits of the labor in the vineyards were not just a source of sustenance but were seen as a direct blessing from God, a tangible sign of His covenant and favor. Similarly, in Catholic tradition, the fruit of the vine holds a special place, transformed into the blood of Christ in the Eucharist, signifying the New Covenant and God's ultimate provision for humanity.

The Feast of Tabernacles was a time when the Israelites would build temporary shelters or booths, reminiscent of those used during their years in the wilderness. This practice was not only a commemoration but also a moment for reflection on one's dependence on God's provision and protection. The Catholic

Church mirrors this reflective practice through the sacrament of the Eucharist, fostering a contemplative heart among the faithful, reminding them of their spiritual journey and God's ever-present protection and provision.

The grape harvest and the celebration of Tabernacles also served as a communal event, strengthening ties within the community and with God. It was a time to recognize that the fruits of the earth and one's labor are not solely from human efforts but are blessings from God, fostering a sense of gratitude and collective responsibility among the people. This communal aspect finds resonance in Catholicism through the celebration of mass, where the faithful gather as a community to partake in the Eucharist, uniting them with Christ and with one another.

Just as the grape harvest required the collective effort of the community, so does the Catholic faith emphasize the importance of communal prayer, support, and celebration. The process of harvesting grapes, pressing them into wine, and then using that wine in the celebration of the Eucharist underscores the interconnectedness of physical and spiritual nourishment, rooted in both individual and communal efforts.

Furthermore, the grape, as a symbol, transcends its physical attributes to embody spiritual truths. In the Catholic Church, the wine represents Christ's blood, shed for the salvation of humanity. This transformative process from grape to wine parallels the spiritual transformation believers undergo through the sacraments, especially the Eucharist. It signifies a transition from the physical to the spiritual, from the earthly to the divine.

Moreover, in the Jewish tradition of Tabernacles, there is a forward-looking aspect, anticipatory of the coming Kingdom of God. This eschatological element is deeply embedded in the Catholic celebration of the Eucharist as well. Each Eucharistic celebration is a proclamation of faith in the Second Coming of Christ, where believers anticipate the fulfillment of God's Kingdom on earth.

The Feast of Tabernacles also highlighted God's provision and the importance of returning to Him in thanksgiving. This sentiment is echoed in the Catholic doctrine of Eucharist, a term originating from the Greek word for thanksgiving. The Eucharist is the supreme act of Christian thanksgiving, a celebration of gratitude for the paschal mystery of Christ, His death, resurrection, and the promise of salvation.

In examining the significance of the grape harvest within the context of the Feast of Tabernacles and its connections to the celebration of the Eucharist in Catholicism, it becomes evident that there is a profound theological and spiritual lineage that links these traditions. The symbolism of the grape and its transformation into wine serves as a powerful metaphor for the spiritual journey of believers, encapsulating themes of community, thanksgiving, provision, and the transformative power of God.

The transition from the agricultural to the spiritual, from the Jewish practice of celebrating the grape harvest during Tabernacles to the central role of wine in the Catholic Eucharist, illustrates the continuation and fulfillment of Jewish traditions within Catholicism. It underscores the Catholic belief in the Church as the fulfillment of the Jewish faith, where the Old Testament practices find their completion and deepest meaning in the New Covenant established by Christ.

This convergence of the Jewish and Catholic traditions offers a pathway for Jewish converts to Catholicism, providing them with a familiar framework within which they can understand and embrace the sacraments, particularly the Eucharist. It invites believers from both faiths to see the continuity rather than discontinuity between Judaism and Catholicism, promoting a greater appreciation for the shared heritage and the unique journey from one to the other.

In sum, the celebration of Tabernacles and the grape harvest holds deep spiritual significance that transcends its agricultural roots, bridging ancient Jewish practices with the core sacramental celebrations of Catholicism. It serves as a testament to the enduring and evolving nature of faith, the interconnectedness of the physical and spiritual worlds, and the unbroken line of divine provision and celebration that ties the Old Covenant with the New.

This exploration not only enriches the understanding of Catholic doctrine and its Judaic roots but also reaffirms the Catholic Church's position as the true continuation and fulfillment of Judaism. It is an invitation to deeper faith, understanding, and unity between two traditions that share much common ground, aimed at fostering a more profound appreciation for the sacramental life at the heart of the Catholic faith.

As we delve deeper into the theological and spiritual parallels between the Feast of Tabernacles and the Catholic Eucharist, it becomes clear that the journey from grape to wine, from Sukkot to the Mass, is a profound expression of God's ongoing relationship with His people. It is a journey that invites all believers to partake in the divine mystery of salvation history, united in a common heritage and a shared hope for the future.

"In the unity of this Eucharist, where the grapes of the vineyard are brought together to become wine, we see the perfect symbol of our unity in Christ, where all are invited to share in the divine life and in the eternal celebration of God's kingdom."

The Sacraments of Initiation in Catholicism

In the vast sea of liturgical practices that constitute the Holy Roman Catholic Church, the sacraments of initiation stand as towering beacons of faith, guiding the faithful on their spiritual voyage from the shadows of sin into the radiant light of grace. These sacraments - Baptism, Confirmation, and the Eucharist - are not merely ceremonial rites; they are the very foundation upon which the edifice of Christian life is built, molding individuals into the likeness of Christ and integrating them into the communal body of the Church.

Baptism serves as the gateway to spiritual rebirth, washing away the original sin inherited from our forebears and bestowing upon us the indelible mark of a new creation in Christ. As the first sacrament of initiation, it symbolizes the death of the old self and the resurrection into a life of grace (Catechism of the Catholic Church, 1994). Through the sanctifying waters of Baptism, the believer is cleansed of all sin and reborn as a child of God, a member of Christ, and a temple of the Holy Spirit, thus initiating the journey of faith that is to be nourished and deepened through the subsequent sacraments.

Following Baptism, Confirmation strengthens this newfound life in the Holy Spirit. It is akin to the Pentecost experience of the Apostles, where the Holy Spirit descended upon them, empowering them to carry out Christ's mission with courage and wisdom (Acts 2:1-4). Through the anointing with chrism and the laying on of hands by the bishop or a designated priest, the confirmed are sealed with the Gift of the Holy Spirit, enabling them to bear witness to their faith with boldness and conviction. This sacrament of initiation further solidifies the believer's commitment to the Church's mission and prepares them for the active participation in the Eucharist.

At the pinnacle of the sacraments of initiation stands the Eucharist, the source and summit of Christian life (Lumen Gentium, 1964). In this sacrament, the faithful partake of the Body and Blood of Christ, entering into a profound union with Him and, by extension, with their fellow believers. The Eucharist is not only spiritual nourishment sustaining the life of grace within but also an anticipation of the heavenly banquet, where the faithful hope to partake in the eternal communion with God. Through these sacred mysteries, Christians are continually formed into the Paschal Mystery of Christ, dying to sin and living for God in Christ Jesus.

The sacraments of initiation, thus, chart the course for the faithful's journey towards full incorporation into the mystical body of Christ, the Church. They lay the foundational stones of a life in grace, enabling the believers to grow in holiness and work for the salvation of the world. In the profound depths of these sacraments, the faithful find the strength to bear witness to the Gospel and to live out the commandments of love, in a world that yearns for the message of hope and salvation.

Baptism: The Doorway to Spiritual Life

The sacrament of Baptism holds a pivotal place within the Catholic Church, marking the beginning of the spiritual journey for every believer. It serves not merely as a ritual of initiation but as a profound transformation, wherein the baptized are cleansed of original sin and reborn as children of God. This transformation is foundational, setting the stage for all other sacraments within the life of a Catholic.

Baptism is often referred to as the 'doorway' to the spiritual life because it initiates the believer into the mystical body of Christ, the Church. This sacrament incorporates the believer into the faith community, making them participants in the divine life. Its significance is deeply rooted in Scripture and tradition, reflecting the Church's understanding of the role of grace and faith in the believer's life.

The act of Baptism involves the use of water, symbolizing cleansing, death, and rebirth. As water washes the body, so does the grace of Baptism cleanse the soul. The ritual echoes the passage of the Israelites through the Red Sea, marking their transition from slavery to freedom, and prefigures our passage from death to life in Christ (Romans 6:3-4). Through this sacramental act, the believer is buried with Christ in death and raised with Him to new life.

In the Catholic tradition, Baptism is more than a symbolic act. It is believed to confer an indelible spiritual mark, or character, signifying the baptized person belongs to Christ. This character, imprinted on the soul, configures the believer to Christ and to the Church, enabling participation in the liturgical life and conferring the capacity to receive the other sacraments.

The universality of Baptism underlines the Catholic Church's mission to evangelize. Christ Himself commanded His disciples to go forth and baptize all nations in the name of the Father, and of the Son, and of the Holy Spirit (Matthew 28:19). This mission underscores the Church's belief in the necessity of Baptism for salvation, a doctrine firmly rooted in Jesus' discourse with Nicodemus (John 3:5).

The tradition of infant Baptism, practiced since the earliest days of the Church, further illustrates the understanding of Baptism as an act of God's grace rather than a human achievement. It is God who initiates and gifts His grace through Baptism, not contingent on the individual's understanding or merit. This practice reaffirms the belief in original sin and the need for divine grace to restore the sanctity lost by Adam and Eve.

The early Church Fathers, drawing from the teachings of the Apostles, underscored the transformative power of Baptism. They saw it as not only a washing away of sin but as a regeneration and renewal by the Holy Spirit. This regeneration is a spiritual rebirth, enabling the baptized to live a new life in Christ and to strive for holiness.

For Jewish converts to Catholicism, Baptism represents the fulfillment of the Old Covenant and the initiation into the New Covenant in Christ. It bridges the gap between the Jewish faith and Catholicism, revealing the continuity and fulfillment of God's salvific plan. The sacrament of Baptism is thus seen as the culmination of God's promise, offering salvation to all, Jew and Gentile alike.

This understanding of Baptism as a means of salvation is deeply entwined with the Catholic view of grace and faith. Grace is considered a free gift from God that enables the believer to respond to His call to holiness and conversion. Faith, in turn, is both a gift and a response, a surrender to the belief in Christ and His teachings. Baptism activates this grace and faith, embedding the believer in the mystery of Christ's death and resurrection.

In the context of the Catholic Church's mission to exalt and propagate the faith, Baptism serves as a testament to the Church's universality and its openness to all who seek God. It embodies the Church's commitment to the spiritual nurturing of its members, initiating them into a lifelong journey of faith and holiness.

Baptism, therefore, is not an end but a beginning. It marks the start of a spiritual journey that spans a lifetime, urging the believer to grow in virtue, to participate actively in the Church's sacramental life, and to engage in the world as a witness to Christ's love and grace.

Through Baptism, the Church affirms the dignity of each person as a child of God, called to share in the divine life. It is a sacrament of inclusion, embracing all who are willing to enter the fold of the Church and embark on the path toward salvation.

Reflecting on Baptism, one is reminded of the profound unity it creates among the faithful. In Baptism, there is neither Jew nor Greek, slave nor free, male nor female; for all are one in Christ Jesus (Galatians 3:28). This unity, forged in the waters of Baptism, is a foretaste of the heavenly banquet to which all the baptized are called.

In conclusion, Baptism stands as the doorway to spiritual life, fundamental to the believer's journey toward God. It encapsulates the essence of the Christian vocation: to die to sin and to live for Christ. As the first of the sacraments of initiation, Baptism lays the foundation for a life of faith, preparing the believer to receive further gifts of grace in Confirmation and the Eucharist. Through Baptism, the Church continues to fulfill

Christ's command, making disciples of all nations and guiding them toward everlasting life.

Confirmation: Strengthening the Spirit

In the continuum of the Sacraments of Initiation within the Catholic Church, Confirmation emerges as a critical juncture, distinct yet deeply interconnected with Baptism and the Eucharist. This sacrament is not merely a rite of passage but a profound deepening of the Holy Spirit's indwelling, initiated at Baptism. It provides the faithful with the strength, gifts, and graces necessary to live out their faith with zeal and courage in the world.

At its core, Confirmation is the sacrament of empowerment by the Holy Spirit. It echoes the Pentecost event when the Apostles received the Holy Spirit and were emboldened to proclaim the Gospel fearlessly. Thus, Confirmation imbues the faithful with a similar spiritual fervor, enabling them to bear witness to their faith (CCC, 1999).

The rite of Confirmation involves the laying on of hands, an act steeped in biblical tradition, symbolizing the bestowal of the Holy Spirit. The anointing with chrism, consecrated oil, signifies the seal of the Holy Spirit, marking the individual as belonging wholly to Christ, charged with spreading and defending the faith. This symbolism finds its roots in the Old Testament, wherein kings, prophets, and priests were anointed for their mission.

In terms of spiritual maturity, Confirmation is akin to reaching a new height. While Baptism removes the stain of original sin, incorporating the individual into Christ's body, Confirmation strengthens this union, enabling the faithful to partake more fully in the mission of the Church. This sacrament, therefore, acts as a bridge, not only between the individual and the divine but also among the community of believers, reinforcing the fabric of the Church.

Confirmation also serves as a reminder that faith is not static but dynamically evolves. The gifts of the Holy Spirit conferred through this sacrament—wisdom, understanding, counsel, fortitude, knowledge, piety, and fear of the Lord—equip the faithful to navigate the complexities of life with grace. These gifts enable individuals to discern the will of God and to act upon it, reflecting the light of Christ in their words and deeds.

It is within this sacrament that the fullness of the Holy Spirit is imparted to individuals, fortifying them in their Christian journey. This fortification is crucial in today's world, where challenges to faith and morality abound. Hence, Confirmation instills not just the courage to resist societal pressures but also the zeal to engage in charitable works, witnessing to the love of Christ.

Theological reflection reveals that Confirmation is the sacrament where the promise of Jesus to send the Advocate, the Holy Spirit, reaches its fulfillment in the believer's life. Therefore, it's an essential component in the believer's spiritual journey, acting as a cornerstone for a mature and active faith life (John 14:16).

In tradition, there is also a deep connection between Confirmation and one's mission in the world. Just as the Apostles were sent out to preach the Gospel, confirmed Christians are charged with specific missions to bring Christ into every area of human life. This underscores the sacrament's missionary character, imbuing life's ordinary moments with extraordinary spiritual significance.

Moreover, Confirmation enriches the individual's bond with the Church, integrating them more fully into its sacred mission. Through this sacrament, believers are called to participate more actively in the Church's liturgy and apostolate, motivated by the Holy Spirit's guidance and strength (CCC, 2002).

Given its profound significance, preparation for Confirmation is undertaken with great care. It involves a period of instruction in the faith, deepening one's understanding of the Church's teachings and the sacraments. This preparation mirrors the journey of the early Church's catechumens, highlighting the continuity of the Church's sacred traditions throughout the ages.

Confirmation's role in the spiritual development of believers highlights the Catholic Church's wisdom in structuring the Sacraments of Initiation to guide the faithful from spiritual rebirth in Baptism through the strengthening of the Spirit in Confirmation, to the sustenance offered by the Eucharist. It is a testament to the Church's understanding of the human need for ongoing spiritual nourishment and growth.

In today's context, where secular influences often lead individuals away from a life of faith, Confirmation stands as a beacon of hope. It offers young Catholics a foundation upon which to build a life that not only adheres to Christian principles but also actively contributes to the preaching of the Gospel.

Therefore, Confirmation is not an endpoint but a beginning. It marks the start of a deeper engagement with one's faith and the broader Christian community. It is a commitment to live out the teachings of Jesus Christ under the guidance of the Holy Spirit, embracing a life of service and evangelization.

Hence, in the grand tapestry of the Catholic faith, Confirmation is a vivid thread, binding the faithful closer to God and each other. It strengthens the spirit for the journey ahead, ensuring that the light of faith burns brightly within the Church and the world.

The Eucharist: Spiritual Nourishment

In the tapestry of Catholic doctrine, the Eucharist stands as a profound testament to spiritual nourishment and divine mystery, a sacrament that sustains the soul on its journey toward communion with God. Distinct from the sacraments of Baptism and Confirmation, which initiate the believer into the life of Christ and fortify them with the Holy Spirit, the Eucharist offers continuous spiritual sustenance. It is in the Eucharist that the believer encounters the true presence of Christ, a miracle that transcends human reason and invites a deeper immersion into the mystery of faith.

The roots of the Eucharist find fertile ground in the Jewish Passover, where the themes of liberation, covenant, and thanksgiving intersect. The Passover meal, rich in symbolism and ancient tradition, prefigures the Last Supper, where Jesus Christ instituted the Eucharist. By breaking the bread and offering the cup, Jesus transcended the Passover's symbolism, inaugurating a new covenant in His blood, one that would pour out salvation for humanity. The Eucharist thus stands as a fulfillment of the Passover, transforming it from a remembrance of past deliverance into a living encounter with the liberating God.

Scientific analysis of the Eucharist reveals a reality that defies empirical measurement. The doctrine of transubstantiation, which states that the bread and wine become the body and blood of Christ while retaining their outward appearances, challenges the parameters of physical science, inviting believers to a faith that sees beyond sight. The Eucharist harbors a divine mystery, one that is deeply rooted in a God who becomes intimately present to His people.

Biblically, the Eucharist is foreshadowed in the manna from heaven and the offering of Melchizedek. These instances reveal a God who nourishes and sustains His people, preluding the ultimate sustenance provided in the Eucharist. In the words of Christ, "I am the bread of life" (John 6:35), believers find the promise of eternal nourishment, a spiritual food that sustains not just the body but the soul unto eternal life.

Theologically, the Eucharist is a sacrifice, a making-present of the once-for-all sacrifice of Christ on the cross. In this divine banquet, the church partakes of the Lamb of God, who takes away the sins of the world. This sacrificial aspect illuminates the depth of God's love, a love that pours itself out for the life of the world. At each Eucharist, the church joins in the heavenly liturgy, entering into communion with saints and angels, celebrating the mystery of faith.

The Eucharist also serves as a call to unity, echoing Jesus' prayer "that they may all be one" (John 17:21). In receiving the Eucharist, believers are united not only with Christ but with one another, forming the Body of Christ, the church. This unity transcends time and space, binding the church to the faithful of all ages in a communion of saints.

Pastoral practice invites believers to frequent reception of the Eucharist. In its nourishment, the faithful find strength for the journey, courage in the face of trial, and a foretaste of the heavenly banquet. It is in the Eucharist that the spiritual life finds its center, a source of grace that transforms and sanctifies the believer.

For Jewish converts to Catholicism, the Eucharist represents both a fulfillment and a new beginning. Just as the manna in the desert prepared God's people for the promised land, the Eucharist prepares believers for the ultimate promised land of heaven. In the Eucharist, Jewish converts find the fulfillment of the Passover, a new covenant meal that brings about communion with the living God.

As a means of salvation, the Eucharist occupies a central place in Catholic soteriology. It is through participation in the Eucharist that the faithful partake of the fruits of Christ's redeeming work. In this sacrament, the church proclaims the mystery of faith:

"Christ has died, Christ is risen, Christ will come again." This proclamation not only memorializes past events but anticipates the future coming of Christ, when the banquet of the Lamb will be celebrated in its fullness.

Understanding the Eucharist requires a synthesis of faith and reason, a heart open to the mystery of God's love. While theological reflection and biblical study can illuminate aspects of this sacrament, its fullness transcends human comprehension. The Eucharist invites believers to an encounter with the divine, a communion that nourishes the soul and prepares it for eternal life with God.

In summary, the Eucharist stands as a central pillar of Catholic faith and practice, a source of spiritual nourishment and divine encounter. It is in this sacrament that the church finds its identity and mission, called to be the Body of Christ in the world. As spiritual nourishment, the Eucharist sustains the believer on the journey of faith, offering strength, unity, and the promise of eternal life. The Eucharist, truly a divine mystery, invites all to the table of the Lord, where heaven and earth meet.

As this section delineates the profound depths and heavenly heights of the Eucharist, may believers be drawn ever deeper into the mystery of faith, finding in the Eucharist the spiritual nourishment that sustains, unites, and sanctifies the church.

Chapter 3: Barley, Wheat, and Grapes: Symbols in Scripture

The sacred texts hold profound depths of meaning, often encapsulated in the simplicity of everyday elements. Among these, barley, wheat, and grapes stand as significant symbols woven throughout scripture. Their presence in the Holy Writ is not merely coincidental or utilitarian but profoundly symbolic, framing the theological and spiritual narrative that bridges Judaism to Catholicism.

Barley, one of the earliest known grains to be domesticated, carries with it themes of beginnings and first fruits. In the Hebrew Bible, barley's role is illuminated during Passover, where it represents the first harvest and symbolizes God's provision and the start of a redemption journey. This theme transitions seamlessly into Catholic thought, embodying the promise of initial faith and baptism, where the soul's journey toward salvation begins.

Wheat follows in this agricultural and symbolic progression. It represents sustenance and abundance, mirroring the spiritual nourishment that comes from a deepening relationship with the Divine. In Catholicism, wheat takes on a profound sacramental presence in the Eucharist, where it becomes the literal and figurative bread of life, echoing Christ's words, "I am the bread of life" (John 6:35). This sacramental bread intimates the transformation from a simple grain to a sustenance of eternal life.

Grapes, and their resultant wine, symbolize joy, celebration, and the culmination of a process. Wine in both Judaic and Catholic liturgies signifies joy and blessing, marking significant moments and transitions. The use of wine in the Eucharist captures the essence of Christ's sacrifice and the outpouring of grace that forms the new covenant—a fulfillment of the promise glimpsed through the grape harvests celebrated during Tabernacles.

The agricultural cycles reflected in these elements underscore a deeper spiritual journey. Barley's early harvest symbolizes the nascent faith of the believer, wheat's abundance points to the growth and sustenance of faith, and grapes signify the maturation of faith culminating in joyous celebration. This progression mirrors the believer's transition from the initial stirrings of faith, through growth and sustenance, to the joy of eternal salvation.

In analyzing these symbols, we unearth layers of theological and spiritual meaning. For instance, the progression from barley to wheat in scriptural narratives can be seen as a metaphor for the soul's maturation—a journey from the simplicity of initial belief to a deeper, more sustaining faith. This metaphor gains even greater depth when considering the Catholic understanding of sacramental grace, where these stages of growth are encountered and nurtured through the sacraments of initiation.

The scriptural references to these symbols and their significance are not random or isolated. They are part of a divine tapestry, woven with purpose and intention. The recurrence of these agricultural products in feasts and rituals, in both Old and New Testaments, underscores the continuity and fulfillment of God's promise. This continuity is a cornerstone of the Catholic faith, which sees itself as the fulfillment of the Judaic tradition.

In this divine economy, nothing is wasted, and every element serves a purpose. Therefore, the study of barley, wheat, and grapes in scripture is not merely academic but offers profound insights into spiritual truths and theological connections between Judaism and Catholicism.

One cannot overlook the importance of these symbols without missing key insights into divine revelation. Their study offers a bridge for understanding, a catalyst for deeper faith, and a testament to the unity and continuity of God's salvific plan.

Through this exploration, we see that the symbols of barley, wheat, and grapes are not only historical references or liturgical materials but are imbued with deep spiritual and theological significance. They are vehicles of divine truth, embodying themes of provision, sustenance, sacrifice, and joy. Their presence in scripture is a testament to the unity of God's plan for salvation, a plan that encompasses both the richness of Judaism and the fulfillment found in Catholicism.

Thus, as we delve deeper into the spiritual symbolism of barley, wheat, and grapes in scripture, we are invited into a more profound reflection on our journey of faith. This reflection bridges ancient traditions and contemporary practice, inviting believers from both Judaic and Catholic backgrounds to see the continuity of their faith journey mirrored in these simple yet profound symbols.

In conclusion, the symbols of barley, wheat, and grapes in scripture serve as more than mere elements of the agricultural life in ancient times. They are deeply rooted in the theological and spiritual narrative that binds Judaism and Catholicism. These symbols offer rich insights into the nature of God's covenant with humanity, the journey of faith, and the promise of salvation. As such, they are central not only to understanding sacred scripture but also to briditing the gap between these two great traditions, underscoring the Catholic Church's role as the fulfillment of the Judaic promise.

Spiritual Significance of Agricultural Products in Ancient Texts

The spiritual significance of barley, wheat, and grapes extends far beyond their value as mere sustenance. In ancient texts, especially within the traditions that flourished in the lands of the Bible, these agricultural products symbolize profound spiritual truths. Understanding their symbolism helps to bridge the gap between ancient rituals and their fulfillment in the Catholic faith.

Barley, considered one of the first grains to be cultivated by humans, holds significant importance in Jewish religious practices. It is associated with Passover, a festival commemorating the Israelites' liberation from Egyptian bondage. This connects barley to themes of freedom and redemption, concepts that are further illuminated in the Christian understanding of salvation through Christ's sacrifice.

Wheat carries its own set of symbolisms. It is the primary grain for making bread, a staple food that sustains life. In the Old Testament, wheat harvests mark the celebration of Pentecost, symbolizing God's provision and the reception of the Torah at Mount Sinai. For Christians, wheat, and by extension, bread, takes on a poignant significance in the Eucharist. This sacrament is seen as the true bread from heaven, Jesus Christ, who nourishes and sustains believers' spiritual lives (John 6:51).

Grapes, and the wine made from them, hold a dual symbolism of joy and suffering. In the Jewish scriptures, wine is often associated with celebration and abundance, notably in festal offerings and the Sabbath. Yet, in Christian scripture, wine embodies the blood of Christ, shed for the forgiveness of sins. This transformation of wine into Christ's blood during the mass is a key aspect of Catholic worship and signifies the new covenant between God and humanity.

The deep connections between these agricultural products and spiritual truths are not coincidental but are woven intentionally into the fabric of scripture. They serve as tangible reminders of divine promises and human responsibilities. For instance, the cycle of sowing and reaping in agriculture mirrors the spiritual journey of growth and purification. This theme resounds in the parable of the sower (Matthew 13:1-23), where the condition of the soil (human hearts) affects the growth of the seed (the word of God).

Intriguingly, these agricultural symbols also highlight the transition from the Old Covenant, established with the Jewish people, to the New Covenant in Christ. Barley and wheat, with their Passover and Pentecost associations, represent the Old

Covenant's promises and their fulfillment in the advent of Christ. The transformation of wine into Christ's blood introduces a new form of communion with God, through the sacrament of the Eucharist. Thus, the Catholic Church views these sacramental elements as the fulfillment of ancient prophecies and practices.

Moreover, the ritualistic use of barley, wheat, and grapes in ancient Jewish feasts underscores the interconnectedness of physical and spiritual nourishment. This interplay is beautifully encapsulated in the Catholic sacraments, particularly the Eucharist, which is both a meal and a divine mystery. The act of consuming bread (wheat) and wine (grapes) is not only a reminder of God's provision but also a participation in the life, death, and resurrection of Jesus Christ.

These symbols, therefore, serve as a bridge, connecting the faith journeys of Jews and Catholics. They reveal the continuity of God's salvific plan through the ages, from ancient Israel to the present-day Church. This continuity reinforces the Catholic belief that Judaism finds its culmination and fulfillment in Catholicism, with Christ at the center of this transformative journey.

In summary, the agricultural products of barley, wheat, and grapes encapsulate deep spiritual significances within both Judaism and Catholicism. They are not mere commodities but vessels of divine truths and mysteries. By delving into their biblical symbolism, believers can gain a richer understanding of their faith and the interconnectedness of the two religious traditions.

For scholars and believers alike, the exploration of these symbols offers a fertile ground for reflection. It invites a contemplation of the ways in which God communicates and fulfills His promises through the tangible elements of creation. As such, these agricultural symbols stand as enduring testament to the ever-present reality of divine grace and the continuation of God's unfolding plan for salvation.

Chapter 4: Passover and Baptism: The Initiation of Faith

The journey of faith for both the Jewish people and Catholics begins with pivotal rituals that mark the initiation into a covenantal relationship with God. For the Jews, this is epitomized in the Passover, a feast that commemorates God's deliverance of the Israelites from Egyptian bondage. Through the Passover, participants reenact and remember the night when the blood of the lamb, smeared on their doorposts, spared them from death. This act of salvation inaugurates their identity as God's chosen people, freeing them to worship Him and live according to His laws (Exodus 12:1-28). Similarly, in Catholicism, Baptism serves as the initial sacrament of faith, where the individual is cleansed of original sin and reborn as a member of the Church, the Body of Christ. Through the waters of Baptism, Catholics enter into a new covenant with God, becoming partakers in His divine life (Catechism of the Catholic Church [CCC], 1992).

At its core, Passover is a ritual of cleansing and rebirth. It signifies the Israelites' transition from slavery to freedom, enabling them to embark on a journey towards the Promised Land. This narrative of liberation and renewal resonates deeply with the symbolism inherent in Baptism. Just as the Israelites passed through the Red Sea, in Baptism, the faithful pass through the waters to emerge reborn. St. Paul in his epistles draws a parallel between these two salvific events, noting that all those who have been baptized into Christ Jesus were baptized into his death and, just like Christ was raised from the dead, so too are we called to walk in newness of life (Romans 6:3-4).

Furthermore, the element of faith plays a crucial role in both rituals. During Passover, the Jewish people's faith in God's promise and His commandments is actualized through their participation in the feast. This collective remembrance strengthens their faith and communal identity. In the Christian context, Baptism is also an act of faith, not only on the part of the individual (or their sponsors in the case of infants) but of the entire Church community that welcomes the new member. It signifies an entrance into a life of faith, rooted in the belief in Christ's death and resurrection, underpinning the Christian's journey towards salvation.

Thus, both Passover and Baptism serve as the initiation rites that define the identity and faith journey of their respective communities. While Passover prepares the Jewish people to live as a community that adheres to the covenant with Yahweh, Baptism integrates the individual into the mystical Body of Christ, initiating a life of grace and sacramental growth. This parallel underscores the Catholic view that the sacraments, particularly Baptism, fulfill the typologies set forth in the Old

Testament, thereby establishing Catholicism as not only the fulfillment of Judaism but also the means of ultimate salvation.

In conclusion, the understanding and appreciation of Passover as the initiation of the Jewish covenant with God enriches the Catholic comprehension of Baptism. It illuminates the sacrament's depth, showing it to be a new covenant that not only washes away original sin but marks the soul for Christ, promising eternal life with God. As such, through the lens of faith, Catholics see in the Jewish Passover a prefiguration of the Christian sacrament of Baptism, both heralding the initiation of a profound relationship with the Divine and the beginning of a journey towards full communion with Him.

Cleansing and Beginning Anew

The journey from Passover to Baptism signifies a profound transition from the old to the new, from bondage to freedom, and from purification to rebirth. This sacramental passage embodies the spiritual metamorphosis that marks the initiation of faith within both the Jewish and Catholic traditions. It's a journey that speaks to the heart of conversion, cleansing, and beginning anew.

In the context of Passover, the theme of cleansing is vividly embodied in the removal of chametz, or leaven, from the home. This act, rich with symbolism, is not merely a physical cleansing but a spiritual preparation, signifying the removal of pride and impurity from the soul (Exodus 12:15-20). It sets the stage for a holy encounter with God, mirroring the inner transformation that accompanies the sacrament of Baptism in Catholicism.

Baptism, for its part, represents the ultimate form of cleansing and new birth. It washes away the original sin and any personal sins, renews the soul, and sanctifies the believer for a new life in Christ (John 3:5). This sacramental act is not just a ritual but an initiation into the mystical body of Christ, the Church. It signifies the death of the old self and the emergence of a new creation (2 Corinthians 5:17).

The parallel between Passover and Baptism is compelling in its depth and richness. Just as the Israelites passed through the Red Sea, leaving behind the slavery of Egypt for the freedom of the Promised Land, so too does the baptismal candidate pass through the waters of Baptism, leaving behind the slavery of sin for the freedom of grace (1 Corinthians 10:1-2).

This transition from Passover to Baptism underscores the fulfillment and continuation of Jewish beliefs within the Catholic faith. It illustrates how the sacraments, particularly that of Baptism, serve as the bridge linking the Old and New Covenants. Here, Catholicism emerges not as a replacement but as a fulfillment of Judaism, embodying the fullness of God's revelation and the promise of salvation.

The purification rites within Judaism, including Passover, undeniably resonate with the cleansing and rebirth offered through Baptism. In both, water plays a central role, symbolizing purification, renewal, and the sustenance of life. Through these rites, believers are invited to experience a spiritual regeneration, to undertake a journey from sin and impurity towards a state of grace and holiness.

This cleansing and new beginning are essential for the initiation of faith, preparing the believer to receive the fullness of God's grace. In Catholicism, this is further nurtured through the sacraments of Confirmation and the Eucharist, which build upon the foundation laid by Baptism. Thus, the initiation process is not a singular event but a journey of continual growth and deepening faith.

The act of cleansing and starting anew is deeply embedded in the spiritual consciousness of both Judaism and Catholicism. It embodies the endless mercy of God, who offers His people countless opportunities for repentence, purification, and a fresh start. This is a divine invitation to leave behind the past, with its sins and failures, and to embrace a future filled with hope, grace, and redemption.

For those transitioning from Judaism to Catholicism, this understanding of cleansing and rebirth offers a harmonious continuity between their ancestral faith and their new spiritual journey. It reassures converts that they are not abandoning their roots but are instead entering into the fuller expression of the faith that has sustained their ancestors.

This journey of initiation, marked by cleansing and beginning anew, highlights the universality of God's call to holiness. It reminds us that, regardless of our paths to faith, we are all invited to be purified, renewed, and united with God. This unity is beautifully expressed through the sacraments, especially

Baptism, which encapsulates the essence of both Passover and the Christian faith.

In reflecting on the profound connections between Passover and Baptism, it becomes evident that the initiation of faith transcends cultural and religious boundaries. It speaks to a deep spiritual longing for purification, renewal, and communion with the Divine. This shared spiritual heritage enriches our understanding of faith and highlights the catholic (universal) nature of God's salvific plan.

Therefore, the journey from Passover to Baptism is not merely a transition between two religious rituals but rather a transformative experience that encompasses the entirety of the believer's life. It's a call to conversion, to a continual turning away from sin and towards God. This ongoing process of conversion is at the heart of both Judaism and Catholicism, reflecting the dynamic nature of faith and the endless mercy of God.

In conclusion, the sacrament of Baptism, much like the Passover, invites the believer to a profound cleansing and a new beginning. This initiation into the faith marks the start of a spiritual journey characterized by growth, transformation, and the deepening of one's relationship with God. It is through this journey that the believer is fully integrated into the mystical body of Christ, realizing the fulfillment of Judaism within the embrace of the Catholic Church.

This narrative of cleansing and beginning anew serves as a powerful testament to the grace that underpins both Passover and Baptism. It invites believers from both traditions to reflect on the commonalities of their faith journeys, recognizing in them the loving hand of God guiding His people towards salvation and holiness.

Pentecost and Confirmation: Empowered by the Spirit

The feast of Pentecost, celebrated fifty days after Passover, holds a pivotal position in both the Judaic and Catholic traditions, marking a moment of profound communal and spiritual renewal. In its original agrarian context, Pentecost commemorated the wheat harvest, symbolizing God's provision and faithfulness. Yet, its spiritual significance was magnified when, according to the Acts of the Apostles, the Holy Spirit descended upon the Apostles, empowering them to preach the Gospel with boldness and clarity (Acts 2:1-4). This transformative event, revered as the birth of the Church, mirrors the sacrament of Confirmation in Catholicism, where the gifts of the Holy Spirit are imparted to believers, fortifying their faith and commissioning them for mission.

Confirmation, as a sacrament of initiation, deepens the grace of baptism, embedding the believer more firmly into the ecclesial community, and bestows upon them the seven gifts of the Holy Spirit: wisdom, understanding, counsel, fortitude, knowledge, piety, and fear of the Lord (Catechism of the Catholic Church, 1994). These gifts are not mere abstract qualities but are tangibly experienced in the lives of the faithful, enabling them to witness to Christ in everyday actions and decisions. This parallels Pentecost's empowering of the Apostles, which was not an end in itself but a means for the worldwide proclamation of the Gospel.

The historic Pentecost and the sacrament of Confirmation both signify moments of profound communal and individual transformation. As Pentecost marked the diversification of God's covenant to include all of humanity through the Apostles' proclamation to the multi-ethnic crowd in Jerusalem, so does Confirmation mark a personal Pentecost for Catholics, empowering them to transcend cultural, linguistic, and societal barriers to embody and preach the universal call to the Kingdom of God. This expansive view of grace and mission further fulfills Judaism by embracing and completing the promise of a blessing to all nations first given to Abraham (Genesis 12:3).

The sacramental theology of Confirmation, encompassing both the indwelling of the Holy Spirit and the commission to apostolic action, finds its biblical roots and validation within the Pentecost narrative, hence establishing a theological and historical continuity between Judaism and Catholicism. This continuity underscores Catholicism's understanding of itself as the fulfillment and extension of Judaism, where the sacraments serve as the means through which the divine promises are actualized in the New Covenant. Thus, the celebration of Pentecost and the sacrament of Confirmation stand as powerful affirmations of the Church's mission to be a light to the nations, drawing all people into the divine harmony.

In conclusion, Pentecost and Confirmation encapsulate the dynamic movement of the Spirit in both communal and personal dimensions, calling believers to a life characterized by spiritual fruitfulness and missionary zeal. By reflecting on these events and rites, Catholics are reminded of their sacred call to participate in God's redemptive work in the world, empowered by the Spirit to bridge the gap between the past promises to Israel and their fulfillment in the global Church. Through this lens, Pentecost and Confirmation not only signify momentous encounters with the Holy Spirit but also serve as enduring reminders of the believer's vital role in the story of salvation, a story that is both deeply rooted in Judaism and brought to its fullness in Catholicism.

The Fruits of the Spirit in the Life of Believers

In delving into the sacrament of Confirmation, we explore how believers are empowered by the Holy Spirit, laying a critical foundation for understanding the manifestation of the Spirit's fruits in the lives of the faithful. As St. Paul delineates in his letter to the Galatians, the fruits of the Spirit encompass love, joy, peace, patience, kindness, goodness, faithfulness, gentleness, and self-control (Galatians 5:22-23). These virtues serve not only as markers of spiritual growth but also as guiding principles for the Christian life.

The infusion of these fruits into the believer's life through the sacrament of Confirmation is the culmination of a transformative journey that begins with Baptism. In this sacramental act, the Holy Spirit descends upon the individual, fortifying them with divine grace to resist sin and adhere to God's will. This empowerment is a continuation and deepening of the grace received through Baptism, designed to perfect what was begun in the first sacrament of initiation.

Confirmation, in essence, is more than a rite of passage; it's a commissioning. It invokes the Holy Spirit to provide the believer with the strength needed to profess and spread the faith both in word and in deed. Thus, the fruits of the Spirit are not mere passive attributes but active expressions of faith that manifest in daily life. These virtues are the hallmarks of a life transformed by the Spirit's power, illustrating the believer's ongoing conversion and sanctification.

The first of these fruits, love, serves as the foundation. It is divine charity that enables believers to love God above all things for His own sake, and our neighbor as ourselves for the love of God. This love is sacrificial and unconditional, mirroring the love Christ has for the Church. It compels us to see the face of Christ in all and to serve Him through serving others.

Joy, the second fruit, is a profound expression of faith that remains steadfast irrespective of trials and tribulations. It is not a fleeting happiness dependent on circumstances but a deep-seated serenity and contentment found in one's relationship with God. This joy is a testament to the believer's trust in God's providence and love, shining forth even in the midst of suffering.

Peace, another fruit, transcends mere absence of conflict. It is the tranquility of order, the calm in the soul that results from being in right relationship with God. This peace which the world cannot give, is a foretaste of the eternal peace promised to us in Heaven. It guides the believer's decisions, fostering reconciliation and unity.

Patience is closely linked to peace, as it entails enduring suffering and trials with a heart anchored in God. It involves trusting in God's timing and His promises, demonstrating a steadfastness that witnesses to the hope we have in Christ.

Kindness and goodness reflect the believer's call to embody the compassion and benevolence of Christ. They involve a genuine concern for the welfare of others, manifesting in acts of generosity, mercy, and love. Through these virtues, believers become a living testament to the Gospel, drawing others to the faith.

Faithfulness, gentleness, and self-control are virtues that govern our actions, thoughts, and desires, aligning them with God's will. Faithfulness keeps us steadfast in our commitment to God. Gentleness, or meekness, reflects Christ's humility and patience towards all. Self-control, a particularly counter-cultural virtue in today's world, enables us to master passions and desires, using them according to God's purposes.

Therefore, the fruits of the Spirit are not just spiritual assets for personal sanctity but also essential tools for evangelical mission. They are evident signs of a believer deeply rooted in Christ, empowered by the Spirit to witness and work for the coming of God's Kingdom. They shape not just individual believers, but through them, the Church's mission in the world.

In practice, these fruits manifest in various ways, from acts of kindness and charity to the perseverance in faith amid persecution. They inspire and sustain the believer's involvement in works of justice, evangelization, and service. In this way, the fruits of the Spirit guide believers to live out their vocation: to be salt of the earth and light of the world (Matthew 5:13-14).

Confirmation, therefore, serves as a critical juncture in the believer's spiritual journey, equipping them with the fruits of the Spirit necessary for their mission in the world. Just as Pentecost marked the beginning of the Church's mission, so too does Confirmation mark a new beginning for each believer, empowered by the same Spirit to continue this mission.

In the broader context of the Church's sacramental life, these fruits enrich the community of faith, knitting believers together in bonds of love, peace, and mutual support. They are signs of the Church's vitality and its fidelity to Christ's command to be witnesses to the ends of the earth (Acts 1:8).

In conclusion, the sacrament of Confirmation empowers believers with the Holy Spirit, enriching them with spiritual fruits crucial for their personal sanctification and their active participation in the Church's apostolic mission. These fruits, manifest in the lives of the faithful, are tangible evidence of the Spirit's presence and activity in the world, calling all to a deeper relationship with God.

Tabernacles and The Eucharist: Communion with the Divine

As we delve into the profound connections between Jewish festivals and Catholic sacraments, it becomes increasingly apparent how the Feast of Tabernacles lays the foundation for understanding the Eucharist's role in achieving communion with the Divine. Historically, the Feast of Tabernacles, or Sukkot, celebrated the final harvest of the year, a period of joy and thanksgiving for the bounty provided by God. This celebration, rich in symbolism and festivity, finds its profound fulfillment in the Catholic Eucharist, an everlasting testament to God's provision and presence amidst His people.

At its core, the Eucharist embodies the culmination of God's saving acts, a sacred tradition transforming the simple fruits of the earth—bread and wine—into the very essence of Christ's body and blood. This metamorphosis echoes the transition from the tangible harvest of Tabernacles to the spiritual nourishment provided through Jesus Christ. As the faithful gather in remembrance, they partake in a divine meal that transcends time and space, uniting them with the infinite.

The theological underpinnings of this connection are deeply rooted in the concept of memorial. Just as the Feast of Tabernacles served as a memorial to the Israelites' journey through the wilderness and God's enduring shelter, the

Eucharist stands as the New Covenant's memorial. Through it, believers remember and partake in Christ's Passion, death, and resurrection, a perpetual offer of salvation to humanity. This memorial is not merely a reflective act but an active participation in the Paschal Mystery, wherein the faithful enter into a mystical communion with Christ and, consequently, the Divine.

Furthermore, the transition from the transient shelters of Sukkot to the permanent indwelling of Christ in the believer highlights a transition from the temporal to the eternal. The booths of Tabernacles symbolized temporary dwelling places, emphasizing mankind's transitory nature and dependence on God. In contrast, the Eucharist initiates believers into an eternal covenant, where the divine presence is not merely visited but resides within. This indwelling transforms the believer, enabling a foretaste of eternal communion with God.

This sacramental communion also nourishes the communal aspect of faith, drawing parallels with the communal celebrations of Sukkot. Just as the Israelites gathered in unity, the Catholic community gathers around the Eucharistic table, reinforcing the Church's unity as the Body of Christ. This communal aspect underscores the sacrament's ability to transcend individualism, fostering a collective identity centered on Christ.

The Eucharist, serving as spiritual nourishment, invokes the imagery of the manna in the wilderness, drawing a direct link to the provisions of Tabernacles. This heavenly bread, which sustained the Israelites, prefigures the Eucharistic bread, which sustains the spiritual life of the believer. Through this sacrament, the faithful are invited to daily rely on the divine provision, a constant reminder of God's care and presence.

The typological reading of Tabernacles in light of the Eucharist reveals a profound reality: the fulfillment of God's promise of salvation through Jesus Christ. The shadow of the old covenant, seen in the agricultural feasts, finds its substance in the new, where the tangible yields to the mystical, and the historical to the eternal.

In conclusion, the transition from Tabernacles to the Eucharist symbolizes the transition from the covenant with Israel to the new covenant with all humankind through Christ. The final harvest, once celebrated with temporary shelters, now finds its fulfillment in the eternal banquet, where believers are called to partake in the divine life. This communion with the Divine, achieved through the Eucharist, is not merely an act of remembrance but an active participation in the divine mystery, offering a foretaste of the heavenly kingdom.

In understanding this profound connection, believers are invited to more deeply appreciate the Eucharist as the culmination of God's saving deeds. Through this sacrament, the journey of faith finds its destination in the eternal embrace of the Divine, a journey that mirrors the progression from the physical harvests of old to the spiritual harvest of souls. As such, the Eucharist stands as a testament to God's enduring love and the fulfillment of the promise of salvation, a beacon of hope for all humanity.

References:

The Final Harvest and Eternal Union

The culmination of the liturgical journey, as articulated in the sacred traditions of Catholicism, finds a profound resonance with the agricultural celebrations of ancient Judaism, particularly in the festival of Tabernacles. This convergence is markedly seen in the celebration of the Eucharist, which stands as the pinnacle of spiritual culmination - the final harvest that leads to eternal union with the Divine.

Within the paradigm of ancient Jewish feasts, the cycle of agricultural harvests - from barley to wheat, and finally to grapes - serves as a metaphor for spiritual progression and fulfillment. The feast of Tabernacles, celebrating the grape harvest, symbolizes the ultimate gathering of nations under the sovereignty of God. Translated into Catholic theology, this imagery finds its fulfillment in the Eucharist, where believers from all nations gather to partake in the body and blood of Christ, culminating in spiritual unity and eternal communion with God.

The sacramental theology of the Eucharist, as taught by the Catholic Church, encapsulates the spiritual nourishment and intimacy with Christ that was prefigured in the gathering and feasting of the Tabernacles. Herein, the faithful partake of the grape, transubstantiated into the blood of Christ, and the wheat, transformed into His body. This act transcends mere memorial; it is a participation in the divine life of Christ Himself, a foretaste of the eternal banquet in the kingdom of heaven.

In the Jewish tradition, the final harvest was a time of joyful celebration and thanksgiving for God's provision. It was a communal affair, emphasizing unity and fellowship among the people of God. Similarly, the Eucharist is a sacramental banquet that not only commemorates Christ's sacrificial love but actively facilitates a communion of believers, uniting them as one body in Christ. Through this union, the Church reflects the universal gathering anticipated in the feast of Tabernacles.

The theological depth of the Eucharist, as an act of thanksgiving and remembrance, echoes the Jewish practice of reciting blessings over the wine and bread. However, in Catholic teaching, these elements carry an ontological transformation, bringing about the real presence of Christ among His people. This profound mystery accentuates the fulfillment of the Tabernacle's symbolism into a reality that surpasses the boundaries of time and space, inviting all humanity into a direct encounter with the divine.

Moreover, the Eucharist serves as an eschatological sign, pointing toward the end times when God will gather His people from every corner of the earth. This eternal union, prophesied in the scriptures and eagerly awaited by the faithful, finds its guarantee and anticipation in every celebration of the Eucharist. As such, it not only looks back to the Last Supper and the Cross but also forward to the heavenly banquet at the end of ages.

For converts from Judaism to Catholicism, the Eucharist embodies the transition from shadow to reality, from anticipation to fulfillment. The rituals and symbols of the old covenant, while profoundly sacred, were but the foretelling of the ultimate sacrifice of Christ on the cross and His perpetual gift of self in the Eucharist. Thus, the final harvest and eternal union promised through the Jewish feasts are graciously received in the fullness of time through the sacrament of the Eucharist.

This theological continuum from the ancient feasts to the Eucharist profoundly illustrates the Catholic Church as the fulfillment of the promises made to Abraham and his descendants. The inclusivity of the final harvest, gathering believers from all nations, manifests the Catholic vision of a universal family of God, united in faith, sacrament, and worship.

In embracing the Eucharist, the faithful are impelled to live out the call to universal fellowship and divine communion. This sacrament compels the believer towards the ethical and spiritual dimensions of Catholic teaching, emphasizing love, service, and sacrifice as reflections of Christ's own life and ministry.

As the Eucharist is celebrated across the globe, it stands as a testament to the fulfilled promise of a new covenant, where the law is written not on tablets of stone but on the hearts of believers. This eternal covenant, sealed by the blood of Christ, inaugurates the final harvest where death is conquered, and life in God is offered to all.

Therefore, the Eucharist, as the culmination of the spiritual journey, fosters not only an intimate union with Christ but also a profound sense of belonging to a community of believers, journeying together towards the promise of eternal life. It is here, at the altar, where heaven and earth meet, that the Catholic faithful participate in the foretaste of the final harvest and eternal union with the Divine.

The celebration of the Eucharist invites the believer into a transformative relationship with Christ, where the fruits of the Spirit are nurtured, and the virtues of faith, hope, and love are perfected. By partaking of this heavenly banquet, the faithful are empowered to bear witness to the Gospel, to serve the least among us, and to advance the kingdom of God on earth as it is in heaven.

It is through this lens that we understand the Eucharist as the fulfillment of the feast of Tabernacles, embodying the final harvest and ushering in the era of eternal union. It represents the culmination of God's salvific plan, weaving the threads of Old and New Testaments into a tapestry of divine love, mercy, and unity.

In conclusion, the final harvest and eternal union, as celebrated in the Eucharist, encapsulates the essence of Catholic faith and worship. It reaffirms the Church's historical and spiritual continuity with Judaism, while simultaneously propelling the faithful towards the eschatological vision of God's kingdom. Through this sacrament, the Church not only commemorates Christ's sacrificial love but also participates in the life-giving mystery of His death and resurrection, fulfilling the ancient longing for communion with the Divine.

References:

The Journey of the Overcomer: From Barley to Wheat

The transition from barley to wheat in the agrarian calendar is not merely a step in the agricultural cycle but serves as a profound metaphor for spiritual maturation. This evolution mirrors the transformative journey that encompasses the transition from Judaism to Catholicism, marking a passage from an initial understanding to a fulfilled faith that encompasses the richness of divine revelation.

Barley, as the first grain to be harvested in the biblical agrarian calendar, symbolizes the initial stages of belief, akin to the early revelations to the Israelites. Just as barley is more tolerant of harsh conditions and less demanding in its cultivation, early faith might not confront the deeper complexities of spiritual understanding. However, this beginning, while vital, is not the culmination of spiritual growth but rather the preparatory phase for a richer, more profound revelation.

Wheat follows barley in the harvest cycle and represents a maturation of faith. It requires more cultivation and attention than barley, symbolizing the deeper, more intricate understanding of God's revelation through Christ and His Church. It stands as a metaphor for the journey from a foundational faith to one enriched by the fullness of Catholic doctrine and the sacraments, specifically the Eucharist, which is often referred to as the "wheat of the elect."

This transformation within the believer, from barley to wheat, is akin to the sacramental journey within Catholicism. Initially, one enters through baptism, cleansed and reborn, much like the barley that signifies the start of the agricultural year and the Passover feast. As we progress in our faith journey, receiving further sacraments, we are strengthened and nourished, matured into wheat ready for the harvest, culminating in the Eucharist.

In examining the transition from Judaism to Catholicism, it's essential to recognize that this journey reflects an expansion upon the foundation laid by Jewish faith practices. The sacraments of the Catholic Church can be seen as the fulfillment and expansion of the Jewish sacrificial system, offering a continuation and deepening of the covenant with God. The Eucharist, in particular, epitomizes this fulfillment, as it brings believers into a profound communion with Christ, mirroring the intimacy of God's relationship with Israel but deepening it through the sacrifice and resurrection of Jesus.

This understanding leads us to see Catholicism not as a replacement but as an unfolding and realization of the promises contained within Judaism. The movement from barley to wheat, thus, does not denote a rejection of the past but a fruition and consummation of what was begun. The journey from Passover to Pentecost, from Exodus to the coming of the Spirit, encapsulates this growth from an initial grasp of faith to its full expression in the Church.

It's pertinent to mention that in agricultural terms, both barley and wheat are essential; one is not superior to the other. Similarly, the spiritual journey from Judaism to Catholicism is not about devaluing one's beginnings but understanding the completion and enrichment of one's faith through the Church.

Faith, as depicted in this metamorphosis from barley to wheat, is dynamic and progressive. It invites an ongoing conversion of heart—a call to continually seek a deeper understanding and integration of the truths revealed by God through His Church. This process of transformation is not mercurial but demands diligent cultivation, echoing the care required to nurture wheat to fruition.

In reflecting upon the Parable of the Sower, we see that the seed—the Word of God—requires fertile soil to grow. The journey of faith, from its barley beginnings to its wheat maturity, is marked by the cultivation of our hearts and minds, allowing the teachings of Christ and His Church to take root and flourish within us.

This spiritual progression is supported by the lived experience of the sacraments, which are not mere rituals but encounters with the living God. They are the means by which we are transformed, by grace, into the likeness of Christ. As wheat must die to bring forth life, so too must we die to ourselves, through penance and self-denial, to live more fully in Christ.

Understanding this transition also necessitates a grappling with the concept of suffering and sacrifice, themes deeply intertwined with both Judaism and Catholicism. Just as the Israelites faced trials in their journey towards the Promised Land, and as wheat must endure the scorching sun to ripen, so too must believers embrace crosses in their quest for spiritual maturity.

Therefore, the journey from barley to wheat is not merely a personal or individual endeavor but a communal one, shared with the Church—the Body of Christ. It is within this community that believers find nourishment, strength, and the means to grow into the full stature of Christ.

In conclusion, the transformation from barley to wheat encapsulates the essence of our spiritual evolution—marked by growth, maturation, and an ever-deepening communion with God through His Church. This journey, steeped in the agricultural motifs of Scripture, offers not only a pathway to understanding the transition from Judaism to Catholicism but also a model for our individual and communal spiritual pilgrimage.

As we ponder this journey, let us be ever mindful of the grace that sustains us and the love that calls us into fuller union with Christ. Through the sacraments, let us be transformed from barley into wheat—nourished, strengthened, and ripe for the harvest of eternal life.

The Transformation Within the Believer

The journey from barley to wheat symbolizes a profound transformation within the believer, a metamorphosis that mirrors the transition from Old to New Covenant, from Judaism to Catholicism. This spiritual evolution is not merely a change of religious affiliation but a profound rebirth of the soul, a purification and strengthening that propels the faithful from the simplicity of barley to the richness of wheat. In essence, it encapsulates the internal change that happens when one embarks on the path of Catholic faith, embracing the sacraments as vehicles of divine grace and truth.

Indeed, this transformation begins with baptism, the sacrament that initiates one into the Christian life (Catechism of the Catholic Church, 1994). Just as barley is the first crop to be harvested, baptism represents the inaugural step in the believer's spiritual journey, cleansing them of original sin and planting the seeds of faith. It's a profound act of rebirth, through which one dies to the old self and rises anew in Christ.

Confirmation furthers this spiritual evolution, akin to the maturation from barley to wheat. It strengthens and solidifies the believer's faith, bestowing upon them the gifts of the Holy Spirit. This sacrament acts as a divine empowerment, enabling the faithful to bear witness to Christ and His Gospel with greater fervor and conviction.

The Eucharist, the pinnacle of Catholic sacraments, nourishes this transformed life. Just as wheat must be ground and baked to become bread, the believer, too, must undergo a form of spiritual refinement. Partaking in the Eucharist, they are united with Christ Himself, sustaining their spiritual journey and drawing them ever closer to the divine.

The internal transformation that occurs within the believer can be likened to the agricultural process of separating wheat from chaff. Just as the wheat must be threshed and winnowed to separate the valuable grain from the worthless husk, so too must the believer undergo a process of purification, shedding worldly desires and attachments to grasp the true essence of faith.

This process of transformation is not instantaneous but evolves over time, nurtured by prayer, sacramental life, and the Word of God. It is a journey that requires perseverance, patience, and trust in the Lord's timing and method of cultivation.

Furthermore, this metamorphosis within the believer echoes the historical transition from Judaism to Catholicism. Just as the sacraments of the Catholic Church fulfill and surpass the ancient Jewish rites, the believer's transformation represents the fulfillment and transcending of their former self. It is a testament to the belief that Catholicism is not a rejection of Judaism but its completion and perfection.

Significantly, this spiritual transformation reflects not only individual growth but also the universal calling of the Church to be a beacon of light to all nations. The transition from barley to wheat symbolizes the Church's mission to gather all people into the fold of Christ, transcending cultural, racial, and religious boundaries.

The journey of the believer, from the simplicity of barley to the richness of wheat, is a powerful narrative of divine grace and human cooperation. It exemplifies the potential for spiritual growth and maturity through adherence to Catholic teachings and reception of the sacraments.

In this light, the transformation within the believer is not merely personal but deeply communal, woven into the fabric of the Church's sacramental life. It underscores the interconnectedness of the Church's members, who, though many, are united in the one body of Christ.

This dynamic process of transformation serves as a compelling invitation to those of the Jewish faith. It reaffirms that the journey into Catholicism is not a departure from their spiritual heritage but an entrance into its fuller expression and realization. The Church beckons them to partake in this metamorphosis, to experience the completion of their faith journey through the sacraments of initiation and growth.

Ultimately, the transformation within the believer is a testament to the power of divine grace working through the sacraments. It stands as a vibrant illustration of the journey of faith, from the partial understanding represented by barley to the fullness of truth symbolized by wheat. It is a journey marked by continuous growth, deepening communion with God, and an unwavering commitment to the mission of the Church.

For those embarked on this spiritual journey, the path from barley to wheat is fraught with challenges and trials. Yet, it is equally lined with moments of grace and profound joy. The transformation within is both an individual and communal enterprise, a testament to the enduring legacy of faith that transcends time and space.

As such, this transformation within the believer is not the end but the beginning of an eternal adventure, one that leads to the ultimate harvest where the faithful are gathered into the granary of heaven. It is a compelling narrative of death and rebirth, of leaving behind old ways to embrace a life of deeper meaning, purpose, and divine intimacy.

In conclusion, the journey of the overcomer, from barley to wheat, offers a rich metaphor for the path of spiritual transformation within the believer. It encapsulates the essence of the Catholic faith, portraying a dynamic process of growth, purification, and ultimate union with the divine. It is a journey that invites all, especially our Jewish brothers and sisters, to witness the fulfillment of ancient promises and embark on a path of renewal and salvation (Logic, 2020)..

Harvests Unfold: The Progression from Jew to Catholic

The seamless transition from Judaism to Catholicism is mirrored in the unfurling of the harvest seasons—an enduring reminder of the divine orchestration behind sacred history. The agricultural feasts, once the heartbeat of Jewish life, find their fulfillment in the sacramental life of the Catholic Church. This majestic journey from Jew to Catholic is both a spiritual passage and a fulfillment of ancient prophecy, woven into the fabric of salvation history.

At the heart of Judaism lie the agricultural feasts: Passover, Pentecost, and Tabernacles, each symbolizing key elements of Israel's covenant relationship with God. They are times of remembrance, celebration, and hope. Similarly, the Catholic Church, through its sacraments of initiation—Baptism, Confirmation, and the Eucharist—offers believers a path of spiritual rebirth, empowerment, and communion.

The transformation from Jew to Catholic is not merely a change of religious affiliation, but an entry into the profound depths of God's salvific plan. It is a progression that has its roots in scripture, where the foreshadowing of Christ's redemptive work is unveiled in the Old Testament and comes to fruition in the New. The sacraments of the Catholic Church are the living continuity of God's promises, a manifestation of the New Covenant prophesied in the ancient texts.

The initiation of faith through Baptism, paralleled by Passover, marks the beginning of this transformational journey. Just as the Israelites crossed the Red Sea into freedom, the Christian believer passes through the waters of Baptism into new life in Christ. This sacramental act of cleansing and rebirth is the doorway to the spiritual life, inaugurating a profound change in the believer's identity and destiny.

Pentecost and Confirmation then share a profound connection, as both signify empowerment by the Holy Spirit. Pentecost marked the giving of the Law and the birth of the Church; similarly, Confirmation strengthens the believer with the gifts of the Holy Spirit, equipping them for a life of faithful witness and service. This empowerment is essential for the progression of the believer from an initiate in faith to an active member of the Body of Christ.

The culmination of this journey is found in the Eucharist, mirrored by the feast of Tabernacles. Just as Tabernacles celebrated the final harvest and God's provision, the Eucharist is the spiritual nourishment of the believers, their communion with Christ, and the foretaste of the heavenly banquet. It is the sacrament that completes the process of spiritual maturation, bringing the faithful into a profound union with God.

Understanding this progression from Jew to Catholic requires a recognition of the fulfilment of scripture in the life and mission of Jesus Christ. He is the paschal lamb, the giver of the Spirit, and the bread of life—realities that the Catholic sacraments make present to the faithful. Through these sacred rituals, the prophecies and symbols of the Old Testament find their completion and ultimate meaning.

This journey of transformation is supported by a rich theological framework that sees Christianity as the continuation and fulfillment of Judaism. The Catholic Church holds that through the sacraments, believers enter into the mysteries of Christ's life, death, and resurrection, thereby participating in the full scope of God's redemptive plan.

The progression from Jew to Catholic, therefore, is not a departure from the faith of Abraham, Isaac, and Jacob, but a deepening of it. It is to embrace the full revelation of God's salvific work through Jesus Christ and to participate in the sacramental life that he instituted for his Church. This understanding serves as a bridge that invites those of Jewish faith to see in Catholicism not a rival religion but the fulfillment of their ancient hope and the continuation of their cherished traditions.

In the final analysis, the transition from Judaism to Catholicism represents a journey from shadow to reality, from type to fulfillment. The feast days of old, with their focus on physical harvests, pointed forward to the spiritual harvests inaugurated by Christ and perpetuated through the sacraments of the Church. Each step in this progression is a revelation of divine love and a call to deeper communion with God.

As Catholics, the invitation is to see in our Jewish brothers and sisters fellow pilgrims on the journey of faith, and to welcome them into the richness of the Catholic tradition, confident that in it lie the fulfillment of the promises made to Israel and the means of salvation for all people.

Indeed, the Church's sacraments offer a way by which the ancient feasts are not only remembered but are also transcended, as believers are invited to partake of the eternal realities they signify. This rich tapestry of divine initiative and human response, of ancient promise and eternal fulfillment, is a testament to the wisdom and providence of God, who guides all things to their appointed end in Christ.

Therefore, the progression from Jew to Catholic is a vital aspect of God's salvific plan—a divine harvest that unfolds through history, bringing together the threads of the Old and New Testaments into a magnificent tapestry of redemption. It is a journey that speaks of fulfillment, of unity, and of the ultimate triumph of divine love.

References:

The Fulfillment of Scripture Through Catholic Sacraments

In tracing the progression from Judaism to Catholicism, one cannot overlook the profound way in which the Catholic sacraments fulfill the Holy Scriptures, echoing the covenantal promises made to the people of Israel. It is within these sacraments that the bridge between the Old and the New Testament finds its strongest arches, offering not only a continuation but a completion of the spiritual journey initiated in Judaism.

Baptism, as the first sacrament of initiation within the Catholic Church, serves as a vivid manifestation of the cleansing rituals found in Judaism. This sacramental act echoes the purification rites of the Jewish faith, yet it extends beyond physical cleanliness, signifying a rebirth into the life of grace—a concept that finds its roots in the symbolism of Passover. Just as the Israelites passed through the Red Sea to freedom from slavery, so does the baptized individual pass from the bondage of original sin into the freedom of God's children.

Confirmation, the second sacrament of initiation, marks the strengthening of the believer's spirit. It can be likened to the Jewish feast of Pentecost, which celebrates the giving of the Law on Mount Sinai. However, in the sacrament of Confirmation, it is not the law but the Holy Spirit that is bestowed upon the believer. This gift empowers the faithful to live out their baptismal promises more fully, echoing the empowerment the Israelites received to follow God's commandments.

The Eucharist stands as the pinnacle of Catholic sacraments, fulfilling the Jewish Passover in a manner that intertwines deeply with Christ's sacrifice. Just as the Passover meal commemorates God's deliverance of the Israelites, the Eucharist commemorates Christ's deliverance of humanity from sin through His death and resurrection. Here, the symbolic elements of bread and wine transcend their earthly origins, becoming the Body and Blood of Christ, thus fulfilling Christ's declaration at the Last Supper.

The sacrament of Reconciliation, or Confession, reflects the Jewish practice of Yom Kippur, the Day of Atonement. However, while Yom Kippur is observed annually, Confession is available to faithful Catholics at any time, offering a continual means of reconciliation with God and community. This sacrament emphasizes God's unlimited mercy and the possibility of returning to grace after sin, a concept deeply rooted in the prophetic writings of the Old Testament.

The Anointing of the Sick, paralleling the healing rituals found in Judaism, underscores the Catholic belief in the sanctity of suffering when united with Christ's. This sacrament, rooted in the compassion and healings of Jesus as recounted in the Gospels, extends the healing power of Christ to the ill and dying, offering not just physical but spiritual healing.

Holy Orders and Matrimony, sacraments of service and communion, echo the covenantal relationships established in the Old Testament. Holy Orders, in particular, can be seen as a fulfillment of the priestly role in ancient Judaism, now expanded in the priesthood of all believers and the unique role of the ordained. Matrimony, reflecting the covenant between God and His people, elevates the marital bond to a sign of divine love and fidelity.

Through these sacraments, the Catholic Church not only continues the spiritual lineage of Judaism but brings it to completion by integrating the promises and symbols of the Old Testament with the fulfillment brought by Christ in the New Testament. This integration points towards the universality of God's salvific plan, which, while originating with the people of Israel, extends to all humanity through the Church.

The sacraments, thus, serve as a profound testimony to the realization of Scriptural promises, embodying God's grace and the continuation of His covenant across the ages. In them, the journey from Jew to Catholic finds its consummation, as the ancient faith of Abraham, Isaac, and Jacob meets its fulfillment in the teachings of Christ, ensuring the continued unfolding of God's salvific plan.

It's essential to recognize that the sacraments are not mere rituals but are actions of Christ Himself. In the Catholic understanding, sacraments are efficacious signs of grace, instituted by Christ and entrusted to the Church, through which divine life is dispensed to us. The Church's role as custodian and dispenser of the sacraments is a testament to its continuation of Christ's ministry on Earth.

This continuity and fulfillment are foundational in dialogues with our Jewish brethren. It illuminates the Catholic faith not as a departure from Judaism but as its divinely intended fulfillment. This perspective is crucial for understanding the sacraments' role in the divine plan, bridging historical faith practices with the eternal truths revealed in Christ.

As the Church teaches, partakes in, and administers these sacraments, it keeps alive the scriptural heritage that forms its bedrock. Through these sacred acts, the ancient promises made to the patriarchs are realized, the prophecies are fulfilled, and the covenant is renewed and made everlasting in Christ.

In conclusion, the Catholic sacraments offer a rich tapestry of salvation history, woven from the threads of both Testaments. They stand as definitive proof of God's unchanging love and His desire for unity with His creation—a unity perfectly manifested in the life, death, and resurrection of Jesus Christ. Thus, the sacraments are not only the fulfillment of Scripture; they are the living continuation of God's promise of salvation to all.

Chapter 9: Converting Hearts: The Catholic Church and Jewish Believers

The Catholic Church, with its rich spiritual and theological heritage, stands as a beacon of hope and salvation. As we explore the journey of converting hearts, particularly from Judaism to Catholicism, we delve into a transformative process underpinned by love, understanding, and a profound respect for the faith journey that each individual undertakes. This chapter is dedicated to unveiling the strategies and considerations involved in nurturing the Jewish believer's transition into the Catholic faith, emphasizing that Catholicism is not a departure from Judaism but its fulfillment and completion.

The Church, in its mission to exalt and propagate the Holy Roman Catholic Faith, recognizes the unique relationship Judaism has with Christianity. The latter does not stand in opposition but is deeply rooted in Jewish tradition, with Christ himself being born into the Jewish faith. This shared heritage forms the foundation of a dialogue aimed at opening hearts to the beauty and truth of the Catholic Church, making evident that Catholicism represents the fullness of the revelation initially bestowed upon the Jewish people.

To foster a sensitive and effective conversion process, the Church advocates a holistic approach that respects the individual's background while guiding them towards the spiritual nourishment found in Catholicism. Integral to this is an understanding of the sacraments as the fulfillment of Jewish rites and feasts, a concept explored in previous chapters. Baptism, Confirmation, and the Eucharist are not merely Christian innovations but the culmination of the spiritual journey begun with the agricultural feasts and rituals of Judaism.

Engagement with Scripture plays a pivotal role in the conversion journey. The Old Testament, revered by both Jews and Catholics, provides a common ground from which to explore the fulfillment of Messianic prophecies in the New Testament. Highlighting these connections helps Jewish individuals see Catholicism not as a rejection of their heritage but as an embrace and completion of the promises deeply ingrained in their scriptural tradition.

Academic discourse, including the contributions of theologians and scholars, enriches this dialogue by offering a well-reasoned and scholarly foundation for the arguments presented. Through rigorous examination and respectful debate, misconceptions can be addressed, and the coherence of Catholic teachings with the essence of Jewish belief can be illuminated. This scholarly approach, reminiscent of the methods of Thomas Aquinas and

Maimonides, allows for an intellectual as well as spiritual exploration of faith.

Furthermore, the personal testimonies of Jewish converts to Catholicism serve as powerful tools of evangelization. These narratives, embodying the lived experience of transition and fulfillment, offer relatable and compelling accounts of the journey towards embracing Catholic truth. They stand as testament to the possibility of a harmonious integration of Jewish heritage with Catholic belief, providing encouragement and a sense of kinship to those considering a similar path.

In facilitating this journey, the Church also recognizes the importance of community. Conversion is not merely an individual endeavor but a communal experience, supported by the fellowship and guidance of the Catholic community. Programs designed to educate and integrate converts play a critical role in nurturing a deep and lasting faith that is both informed and experiential.

In conclusion, the mission of converting hearts from Judaism to Catholicism is approached with a spirit of love, respect, and a profound belief in the continuity of faith that Catholicism offers. By respecting the individual's journey, engaging in academic and scriptural dialogue, sharing personal testimonies, and fostering community support, the Church strives to illuminate the path towards salvation found in the embrace of Catholicism.

As we progress towards a deeper understanding and respect between these two faith traditions, it is imperative that the dialogue remains anchored in the shared heritage and the fulfillment of promises that bind us. Conversion, therefore, is not seen as a departure but as a homecoming to the fullness of faith that Christ offers to all, opening the door to an eternity of communion with the Divine.

Strategies and Considerations in Faith Conversion

The process of converting hearts from Judaism to Catholicism is a journey marked not only by intellectual assent but also by deep spiritual transformation. This chapter aims to explore the strategic and thoughtful approaches that can facilitate this beautiful transition. It's essential to understand that the essence of conversion goes beyond merely changing one's religious affiliation; it's an invitation into a deeper relationship with God through the fullness of truth found in the Catholic Church.

Firstly, it's crucial to approach each individual with profound respect and sensitivity. The journey from Judaism to Catholicism is deeply personal and can be fraught with emotional, cultural, and spiritual challenges. Recognizing the rich religious heritage that Judaism offers, the Church must present itself as the fulfillment of this ancient faith, rather than its negation. This acknowledgment paves the way for open and honest dialogue (Vatican II, 1965).

At the heart of effective evangelization is the demonstration of genuine love and concern. Pope Francis has emphasized the importance of encounter and accompanying individuals on their spiritual journey with compassion and understanding. This relational approach can break down barriers of resistance and open doors to fruitful discussions about faith.

It is also beneficial to draw parallels between Jewish and Catholic beliefs, highlighting the continuity between the Old and New Covenants. Emphasizing the Jewish roots of the Catholic faith can be a powerful tool in demonstrating the organic development of divine revelation. This connection can help Jewish individuals see Catholicism not as an alien or opposing faith, but as the fulfillment of the promises made to their ancestors.

Scripture plays a pivotal role in the conversion process. Many Jews hold a deep reverence for the Hebrew Scriptures. By engaging in thoughtful scriptural study together, one can gently point out the typologies and prophecies within the Old Testament that find their fulfillment in Christ and the Church. Such discussions can illuminate the Catholic faith as the natural heir of biblical Judaism.

Introducing Jewish individuals to the beauty of the Catholic liturgy, especially the Eucharist, is another powerful approach. The Passover Seder, with its profound symbolism and salvific narrative, finds its perfect fulfillment in the Mass. Explaining the connections between these sacred rites can awaken a longing for the Eucharistic feast, which is the source and summit of our faith (Catechism of the Catholic Church, 1992).

Providing testimonies of other Jews who have embraced Catholicism can offer encouragement and a sense of solidarity. Hearing the stories of those who have navigated the complex path from Judaism to Catholicism can inspire and offer practical insights into the journey ahead.

Patience is key in the conversion process. Spiritual growth cannot be hurried and each individual's journey is unique. It's important to respect God's timing in their life, offering support and guidance, without pressure or coercion.

The role of prayer cannot be overstated in the work of conversion. The power of prayer in opening hearts and minds to the truth of the Gospel has been witnessed throughout the history of the Church. Praying with and for those considering conversion invites the Holy Spirit to work within their hearts, guiding them gently towards the fullness of truth.

Encouraging participation in community life within the Church can be very effective. The warmth and welcoming nature of Catholic community life can provide a tangible experience of Christian love and fellowship, contrasting with the often intellectual approach to faith found in Judaism.

Finally, it's important to offer robust catechetical instruction that deepens understanding and appreciation of the Catholic faith. This teaching should be intelligible and relevant, addressing common questions and concerns from a Jewish perspective.

Conversion is ultimately the work of God, and the Church's role is to cooperate with grace, sowing seeds of faith that the Holy Spirit can nurture into full bloom. Through thoughtful engagement, respectful dialogue, and loving witness, the Catholic Church can successfully guide Jewish believers towards embracing the beauty and truth of Catholicism, affirming its position as the fulfillment of Judaism and the means of salvation.

Sacramental Theology: Understanding Divine Grace

In the journey of faith, the Catholic Church holds that its seven sacraments are the manifestation of divine grace, acting as conduits through which the faithful receive sanctifying grace—an essential element for salvation. This theological standpoint is not merely a ritualistic practice but a profound explication of the divine economy of salvation, where God's grace is freely bestowed upon humanity. In understanding sacramental theology, it's crucial to grasp that these sacred rites are not symbolic gestures; rather, they are actual means by which divine life is dispensed to the faithful (Vatican II, 1964). The role of sacraments in salvation underscores the Church's belief in the tangible and transformative presence of God's grace in the life of every believer.

At the heart of sacramental theology is the concept of 'ex opere operato,' implying that the sacraments confer grace when performed in their proper form by the Church, irrespective of the personal holiness of either the minister or the recipient. This principle upholds the objective efficacy of sacraments, ensuring that God's grace is accessible to all believers, thus facilitating a universal pathway towards redemption and union with God. Through this understanding, the Church asserts that the sacraments, instituted by Christ Himself, serve as the foundational elements in the life of the Church, deeply entwining the physical and spiritual realms (Catechism of the Catholic Church, 1992).

The sacraments are celebrated as both communal and personal encounters with the divine, reinforcing the unity of the Church while fostering individual spiritual growth. They stand as the fulcrum around which the believer's life pivots, marking significant spiritual milestones and nurturing the soul on its journey towards sanctification. In essence, sacramental theology articulates a vision of the Church as a vessel of divine grace, wherein the sacraments act as the very lifelines of spiritual life, offering a foretaste of the eternal banquet in the heavenly Jerusalem. Thus, diving deep into sacramental theology is not just an academic exercise but a journey into the heart of divine grace, unfolding the mystery of God's love and mercy towards humanity.

The Role of Sacraments in Salvation

The sacraments, instituted by Christ Himself, are vital to understanding the Catholic Church's teaching on the process of salvation. To appreciate their significance, it is essential to delve into the essence of sacramental theology, with a special emphasis on how these sacred rites serve as conduits of divine grace, heralding a transformative journey towards salvation. As outlined in the previous chapters, the analogy between Jewish feasts and Catholic sacraments unveils a profound continuity in God's salvific plan.

At the heart of sacramental theology is the assertion that sacraments are not mere symbols; they are efficacious signs instituted by Christ that confer the grace they signify. This foundational belief hearkens back to the chosen people's covenantal signs with God, manifesting a trajectory from the Old Covenant to the New Covenant fulfilled in Christ. Hence, the sacraments operate as the New Law's channels, through which the salvific grace of Jesus Christ flows into the lives of believers.

Sacraments serve a dual purpose in the economy of salvation: they sanctify individuals, incorporating them into the Body of Christ, and serve as the liturgical worship pinnacle, uniting heaven and earth in a cosmic liturgy. This understanding is paramount for Roman Catholics, Biblical scholars, university professors and students, and Jewish converts to Catholicism, illuminating the sacraments' role in personal and communal salvation.

Baptism, as the initial sacrament of initiation, holds a prime position in the believer's spiritual journey. It signifies and effects regeneration and incorporation into Christ's mystical body, the Church. Drawing parallels to the Jewish Passover, baptism represents a passage from bondage to freedom, from death to life, echoing Israel's exodus and pointing to the Christian's rebirth (John 3:5). The water used in baptism symbolizes purification, but, through the Trinitarian formula, it effectuates the reborn individual's adoption as God's child.

Confirmation, another sacrament of initiation, strengthens and deepens the grace imparted at baptism, equipping believers with the Holy Spirit's gifts for mature witness to Christ in word and deed. This sacrament finds its roots in the Jewish feast of Pentecost, symbolizing the descent of the Holy Spirit upon the apostles. Confirmation empowers Catholics to be active participants in the Church's apostolic mission, embodying the faith courageously.

The Eucharist stands as the summit of the Church's sacramental life. It perpetuates the sacrifice of the cross, renders it present in every celebration, and effects communion with Christ and, through Him, with the entire Church. The bread and wine, becoming Christ's Body and Blood, recall the offerings of the Jewish Temple but transcend them, offering the very life of God to the faithful. The Eucharist consummates the spiritual journey begun in baptism and strengthened in confirmation, drawing believers into the divine life.

This sacramental approach to salvation underscores a pivotal shift from the Old Covenant's observances to the New Covenant's mysteries. Where the former prepared the way, the latter accomplishes and actualizes salvation history, fulfilling God's promise of redemption. The sacraments, as the primary means of grace, are indispensable for salvation, sanctifying believers and binding them more closely to the life and mission of Christ.

The reconciliation of God and humanity, effected through Christ's sacrifice, finds its tangible and continued application in the sacrament of Confession. This sacrament, by allowing repentance and absolution of sins, mirrors the mercy God showed to Israel, calling her to conversion through the prophets. Confession restores the grace lost by sin, reconciling believers with the Church and renewing their journey towards salvation.

Holy Orders and Matrimony, sacraments at the service of communion and mission, facilitate the faithful's vocational response to God's call. Holy Orders perpetuate Christ's priestly mission, enabling a sacramental representation of Christ as head of the Church. Matrimony, reflecting the covenantal love between God and Israel, elevates the union between a man and a woman to a sign of divine love and a means of grace.

The sacrament of Anointing of the Sick, by conferring grace for the spiritual and, if God wills, physical healing, embodies the Church's ministry to the suffering, as Jesus did. It completes the sanctification of those nearing their earthly journey's end, preparing them for eternal life. This sacrament, in continuity with Jesus' healing miracles, constitutes a profound expression of faith in God's power to save and to sanctify through suffering.

In embracing the sacraments, Catholics participate intimately in the paschal mystery of Christ. Each sacrament, in its unique way, makes present the salvific deeds of Jesus' life, death, and resurrection, allowing the faithful to draw from the wellspring of grace needed for the journey towards full communion with God. Through them, the Church lives as the sacrament of salvation for the world, visibly expressing and effecting the mystery of God's love.

For Jewish converts to Catholicism, recognizing the fulfillment of Judaism in the sacramental life of the Church can be a profound revelation. The continuity from the Old to the New Covenant elucidates the divine plan for humanity's redemption, offering a comprehensive understanding of God's salvific intention. The sacraments, as tangible expressions of this divine mercy, mark the path from the shadows of the Law to the radiant light of Grace.

Thus, the role of sacraments in salvation is not only foundational but also transformative. They are not static rites but dynamic encounters with Christ, the living God, who continues to act in and through His Church. As the Church upholds and administers these sacred mysteries, she fulfills her mission as the bearer of divine grace, guiding souls on their pilgrimage towards the heavenly Jerusalem.

Engaging in sacramental life, therefore, is essential for the salvation of the believer. It is not a mere adherence to ritual but an invitation to partake of the divine nature (2 Peter 1:4). The sacraments, in their essence and operation, signify and realize an intimate communion with God, effected by Christ and sustained by the Holy Spirit, leading the faithful towards their ultimate vocation: eternal life with the Triune God.

In conclusion, the sacraments hold a central place in the Catholic understanding of salvation. By participating in these rites, believers are drawn into the very life of God, initiated into a personal and communal relationship with Christ, and equipped for their role in the Church's mission. The sacramental liturgy, thus, stands as a beacon of hope, a foretaste of the heavenly banquet to which all are called.

Chapter 11: Debating Theology: Addressing Common Objections and Misunderstandings

In progressing through an exploration of the connections between Judaism and Catholicism, we've traversed a significant theological and spiritual landscape. As we delve deeper into the essence of our faith journey in this chapter, it becomes crucial to address some common objections and misunderstandings that arise when debating theology, especially between these two deeply connected yet distinct faith traditions.

One of the first points of contention often revolves around the concept of the Messiah. Within Judaism, the expectation of a Messiah is a fundamental aspect, one that is often seen as unfulfilled. However, from the Catholic perspective, Jesus Christ embodies the fulfillment of these Messianic prophecies. This divergence in belief can lead to significant theological debate. To address such concerns, it's essential to analyze the prophecies within the Hebrew Scriptures through a lens that accounts for both immediate and typological fulfillments, demonstrating how Christ's life, death, and resurrection correspond intricately to the Messianic expectations outlined in texts such as Isaiah 53 and Psalm 22.

Another frequent objection pertains to the Catholic veneration of Mary and the saints, which some from the Jewish faith may misconstrue as a form of idolatry. It's important to clarify that within Catholic theology, veneration (dulia) significantly differs from the worship (latria) due only to God. The saints, and Mary as the Queen of Saints, are honored as exemplars of faith and intercessors, not as deities. This distinction, rooted in the Communion of Saints, speaks to the understanding that the Church is not bound by death and that those in heaven continue to be part of the community of faith (Catechism of the Catholic Church, 1994).

Concerns are also raised regarding the Catholic approach to scripture and tradition. Critics may argue that Catholicism places undue emphasis on Church tradition, overshadowing the authority of the Hebrew Bible and the New Testament. Yet, this perspective overlooks the Catholic teaching that Scripture and Tradition are not competing sources of revelation but rather complementary. The Tradition of the Church, consisting of teachings handed down from the apostles under the guidance of the Holy Spirit, provides a lived context that illuminates and interprets Scripture (Dei Verbum, 1965).

Practices such as the sacraments, especially the Eucharist, are sometimes viewed with skepticism due to their sacramental and sacrificial nature, which may seem alien or even contrary to Jewish understandings of worship and sacrifice. However, when seen through the lens of fulfillment and continuation, it's clear that these sacraments, particularly the Eucharist, serve as the New Covenant's realization of Passover. Just as Passover celebrated deliverance and covenantal renewal in Judaism, the Eucharist celebrates and makes present the new deliverance and covenant established by Christ's sacrifice (1 Corinthians 5:7).

Debates around these issues are not merely academic or theological in nature; they touch upon deeply held beliefs and convictions. Engaging with these concerns respectfully and thoughtfully, therefore, is not only a matter of intellectual discourse but also a pastoral necessity. When addressing such objections, the goal is not to "win" arguments but to invite deeper understanding and dialogue. This approach aligns with the Catholic Church's commitment to ecumenism and interfaith dialogue, emphasizing mutual respect, understanding, and the pursuit of truth.

In response to Jewish queries on Catholic practices, it is also crucial to delve into the historical context in which Christian beliefs and practices developed. Understanding the Second Temple Judaism milieu out of which Christianity emerged helps explain how early Christians, many of whom were Jewish, could see in Jesus the fulfillment of their theological expectations, and how practices such as the veneration of saints could develop within a monotheistic faith.

Moreover, considerations of shared heritage and differing interpretations lead to fruitful discussions rather than insurmountable divisions. By acknowledging our common roots and the profound interconnectedness of our faith traditions, we foster a dialogue that transcends mere theological debate, aiming instead for a deeper appreciation of our shared history and differing paths.

In conclusion, addressing common objections and misunderstandings in the realm of theology, especially between Judaism and Catholicism, requires a nuanced understanding of each faith's teachings, a respect for their unique perspectives, and a commitment to dialogue rooted in charity and truth. Through such exchanges, we not only clarify misconceptions but also illuminate the rich tapestry of belief that unites and distinguishes our faith traditions.

As we move forward, it remains crucial to continue these conversations with openness, respect, and a sincere desire for mutual understanding. In doing so, we honor our heritage, enrich our faith, and pave the way for a future marked by deeper dialogue and understanding between Jews and Catholics.

Jewish Queries on Catholic Practices

In engaging with the theological dialogues that bridge Judaism and Catholicism, one identifies a rich, complex interplay of beliefs and practices that have both united and divided these faith traditions over millennia. As we delve into the common queries posed by our Jewish brothers and sisters regarding Catholic practices, it's essential to approach these matters with both a spirit of humility and an earnest quest for truth.

One prominent question concerns the Catholic veneration of images, which can seem to contravene the Second Commandment's prohibition against graven images. It's crucial to clarify that Catholics do not worship these images but employ them as visual aids to focus their veneration on God and the saints. Just as photos of loved ones remind us of their presence and evoke love, so too do religious images in Catholicism serve as gateways to the divine, aiding in meditation and prayer, not serving as objects of worship themselves.

The sacrament of Baptism often raises questions, particularly regarding its administration to infants. Here, understanding is rooted in the New Testament's depiction of Baptism not merely as a symbolic act but as a necessary initiation into the life of grace and salvation (see, for example, John 3:5). The practice of infant baptism is seen as a continuation of the Jewish tradition of circumcision—an entry point into the covenant with God, now opened to all, regardless of age, through Jesus Christ.

Another area of inquiry is the Catholic Mass, especially its claim to re-present the sacrifice of Christ. To elucidate, the Mass does not re-sacrifice Christ; rather, it makes present the one eternal sacrifice of Christ on the cross in a non-bloody manner. This concept finds its roots in the understanding of God's timelessness, where Christ's sacrifice transcends time and space, making it present to believers now.

Confession, or the Sacrament of Reconciliation, is another practice sometimes questioned. It's based on Jesus' post-resurrection appearance to his disciples, where he empowered them to forgive sins (John 20:23). This sacrament provides a profound encounter with God's mercy, inviting a personal and communal purification that enriches the community of faith.

The role of Mary and the saints in Catholicism often perplexes many from a Jewish background. Far from taking away from the centrality of God, the veneration of Mary and the saints reflects the biblical teaching on the communion of saints—believers are connected in Christ, whether in heaven or on earth. The intercession of the saints is seen not as a form of divination but as an extension of the familial bond among God's people, asking a beloved family member to pray "for us," much as one would on earth.

The doctrine of the Trinity, encapsulating the Father, the Son, and the Holy Spirit as one God in three persons, is another aspect frequently subject to misunderstanding. This belief is rooted in the scriptural revelation of God's nature, as evidenced in the baptismal formula prescribed by Jesus (Matthew 28:19) and the Pauline benedictions (2 Corinthians 13:14). The Trinity represents the maximum expression of God's self-revelation, a mystery that, while beyond full human comprehension, is accessible through faith and reason.

Purgatory, often misunderstood, is not a second-chance destination but a purification process for those who die in God's grace and are assured of their eternal salvation yet require purification to enter into the fullness of God's presence. This doctrine underscores God's mercy and justice, providing a deeper understanding of the communal nature of salvation. It echoes the Jewish practice of praying for the dead, an acknowledgment of the ongoing journey of the soul towards perfection.

Finally, the Catholic Church's claim to authority, particularly through the papacy, can be a point of contention. This claim is grounded in the biblical mandate given by Christ to Peter, whom

Catholics regard as the first pope, when Jesus said, "You are Peter, and upon this rock, I will build my church" (Matthew 16:18). The papacy is not a human invention but a divinely instituted office for the unity and continuity of Christ's teachings through the ages.

In addressing these queries, our aim is not merely to assert Catholic truth but to invite deeper reflection on how Catholic practices embody the full revelation of God's salvific plan. It's in the spirit of honest and respectful dialogue that true understanding can emerge, providing a bridge between our cherished Jewish roots and the fulfillment Catholics find in Christ.

Engagements of this nature are not just theological exercises but are profound invitations to spiritual communion, echoing the universal call to unity in truth and charity. It's through such earnest and informed dialogue that misconceptions can be clarified, and the full beauty of Catholicism can shine forth as the fulfillment of Judaism's ancient promises.

As we move forward in understanding, let us always remain anchored in love and respect for our faith traditions, recognizing in them the unique paths to encountering the Divine that have been trod by faithful seekers across ages. It's in this journey towards truth and understanding that we find our common heritage and potential for profound spiritual solidarity.

References:

Catholic Responses to Jewish Concerns

In addressing the concerns raised by our Jewish brothers and sisters regarding the Catholic faith, it's crucial to approach these discussions with respect, understanding, and an earnest desire for truth. Many questions arise from misconceptions or genuine curiosity about how Catholicism relates to or fulfills Judaism.

One common concern is the Catholic veneration of statues and images, which can be misconstrued as idolatry. It's important to clarify that Catholics do not worship these images but use them as visual reminders of God's presence and the saints' exemplary lives. Just as the Ark of the Covenant was adorned with cherubim (Exodus 25:18-22) without violating the commandment against idolatry, so too does the Church use sacred art to lift the mind to divine realities.

Another significant point of discussion is the concept of the Trinity, which may seem to contradict the Jewish affirmation of God's absolute unity. The Church teaches that God is one in essence but three in persons - Father, Son, and Holy Spirit. This mystery of faith does not divide God's unity but rather reveals His inner life and love. The seeds of this understanding can be seen in the Shema's declaration of God's oneness (Deuteronomy 6:4) paired with the plural references to God found in Genesis

1:26 and Psalms 110:1, hinting at a complexity within God's unity.

Regarding the Messiah, many Jewish people expect a political leader who will restore Israel to greatness. However, Christians believe Jesus Christ fulfills the messianic prophecies through His spiritual kingdom, which transcends earthly boundaries and unites all people in love and truth. Isaiah's prophecy of a suffering servant who bears our iniquities (Isaiah 53) aligns with Christ's sacrificial love, demonstrating how Jesus embodies the true Messiah who liberates humanity not from political oppression but from the bondage of sin.

The Catholic understanding of salvation can also be a stumbling block. While some may view the Catholic emphasis on sacraments and works as diverging from Judaism's focus on faith and obedience to the Law, it's essential to recognize that these elements are not in opposition. Catholics believe that faith and works are two sides of the same coin - faith inspires works, and works demonstrate and deepen one's faith. James 2:24 supports this synthesis, showing how faith is perfected by works, echoing the holistic view of faith and actions found in Jewish scripture.

The role of Mary, the mother of Jesus, often raises questions. Catholics honor Mary as the mother of God, given her role in salvation history, but do not worship her as divine. This veneration is akin to the respect paid to the matriarchs and heroines in Jewish history. Mary's "Fiat" (her yes to God's plan) in Luke 1:38 mirrors the obedience and faithfulness of figures like Esther and Judith, showcasing the pivotal role of women in God's salvation plan.

Additionally, the concept of the New Covenant can be a source of tension. It's critical to understand that the Church sees this covenant, established by Jesus, not as abolishing the Mosaic Law but as fulfilling and perfecting it (Matthew 5:17). The New Covenant brings to completion the promises made to Abraham and through Moses, offering a universal call to salvation that extends beyond ethnic and cultural boundaries to embrace all of humanity.

The Eucharist, as the source and summit of Catholic life, may also be perplexing. However, when viewed through the lens of Passover, the similarities become more apparent. Just as the Passover meal commemorates and makes present the Exodus and God's deliverance, so too does the Eucharist commemorate and make present the New Passover of Christ's Sacrifice, delivering humanity from sin and death.

In conclusion, while there are undoubtedly differences between Jewish and Catholic beliefs, there is also profound respect and a shared foundation. The Catholic Church sees itself as the fulfillment of the promises made to Israel, a continuation and deepening of the one faith in the God of Abraham, Isaac, and Jacob. Our discussions should always aim towards understanding, respect, and the shared pursuit of truth that binds us together.

The Promise of Salvation: Catholicism as the Continuation of Judaism

In the progression of faith traditions, the relationship between Judaism and Catholicism presents a profound continuum of divine revelation and salvation history. The course of religious history reveals that Catholicism, with its sacraments and teachings, not only emerges from the roots of Judaism but also reaches its fulfillment in Christ, promising salvation to all people, including the Jews, through a new covenant.

The Old Testament, revered by both Jews and Catholics, speaks volumes of the coming Messiah and the establishment of a new covenant. These prophecies, found in scriptures such as Jeremiah 31:31-34, illuminate the transition from the Mosaic covenant, centered on the law, to the new covenant, centered on grace and faith in Jesus Christ. This transition is not a replacement but a continuation of God's promise to His people.

The notion of salvation holds a central place in the narratives of both religions, wherein lies the core argument for Catholicism as the fulfillment of Judaism. It's imperative to understand that this fulfillment does not imply supersessionism but rather an evolution or maturation of divine revelation. Salvation, once confined to the observance of the Torah and sacrificial rites, is now accessible through the sacrifice of Christ, acknowledged as the Lamb of God (John 1:29).

Jerusalem, a sacred city for both faiths, symbolizes this profound connection. The very geography that hosted the ancient Jewish temple, wherein sacrifices were made for the atonement of sins, later witnessed the ultimate sacrifice of Jesus Christ. This sacrifice on Calvary signifies the new, eternal covenant offering salvation to all, an extension of God's promise to Abraham and his descendants.

The sacraments of Catholicism, especially the Eucharist, find their prefiguration in the Jewish Passover meal. Just as the Israelites remembered their deliverance from Egypt by God's hand during Passover, Catholics remember and participate in the sacrifice of Christ through the Eucharist. This continuity in memorial practice underscores the seamless transition from Jewish tradition to Catholic fulfillment.

Furthermore, the early Christian Church, as depicted in the Acts of the Apostles, was predominantly Jewish in its initial followers and practices. The apostles, all Jewish, were the first to receive the Holy Spirit, marking the birth of the Church at Pentecost. This event mirrors the Jewish feast of Shavuot, further illustrating Catholicism's roots in Judaism.

Conversion of the heart, a concept familiar to both traditions, takes on new meaning in Catholicism. The call for conversion among Jews is not a call away from their ancestral faith but a deepening of it. Embracing Catholicism means recognizing the fulfillment of the Jewish hope in Christ's coming and the establishment of a new covenant not written on stone, but upon the heart (Hebrews 8:10).

In dialogue with Jewish brothers and sisters, Catholics must approach with deep respect and love, recognizing the shared heritage. The Church teaches that God's covenant with the Jewish people is irrevocable (Romans 11:29), thereby establishing a continuous link between Judaism and Catholicism.

Understanding the sacraments as the fulfillment of Jewish signs helps illuminate the path from the old to the new covenant. For instance, baptism in Catholicism is prefigured by various purification rites in Judaism, but it furthers the meaning to a spiritual rebirth and cleansing from original sin.

Contemplation on the Blessed Virgin Mary, revered profoundly in Catholicism, offers another bridge. As a Jewish maiden chosen to bear the Messiah, Mary epitomizes the perfect synthesis of Judaism and Catholicism. Her "fiat" (Luke 1:38) underscores the obedience to God's will, a virtue deeply enshrined in both faiths.

Salvation history, as viewed through the lens of Catholicism, is a narrative of continuity, fulfillment, and hope. The Church sees herself as the "new Israel," not in a way that discards the "old" but rather fulfills it. This vision of fulfillment extends an invitation to all, especially our Jewish brothers and sisters, to partake in the promises of Christ.

Debates and discussions between Judaism and Catholicism concerning salvation must then focus not on contention but on understanding and mutual respect. It's through these dialogues that deeper truths are uncovered, fostering a greater appreciation of both faith's contributions to the understanding of salvation.

The promise of salvation, articulated through Catholicism, stands as an open invitation to all, providing a means to eternal union with God. It underscores the belief that through Christ, the barriers between Jew and Gentile have been dissolved, ushering in a new era of salvation history where all humankind is called to unity with the divine.

In conclusion, Catholicism's understanding of itself as the continuation of Judaism offers a profound perspective on salvation history. This theological stance pays homage to its Jewish roots while advancing the narrative of salvation through

Christ. Together, both faiths stand as witnesses to the unfathomable depth of God's love and mercy towards humanity.

Theological Justification for Conversion

The journey of faith from Judaism to Catholicism stands on profound theological foundations that encompass the promise of salvation. These foundations pave the way for understanding Catholicism not as a separate entity, but as the fulfillment of the covenantal promises made by God to His chosen people, Israel. This theological justification for conversion, deeply embedded in scripture and tradition, illuminates the path for Jews to embrace the Catholic faith as the continuum of God's salvific plan.

At the heart of this theological discourse is the concept of Jesus Christ as the Messiah, long awaited in Jewish prophecy. The prophecies of Isaiah, Jeremiah, and Daniel, among others, foretell a Messiah who would establish a new covenant, not just with the Jewish people, but with all of humanity. Catholic theology posits that Jesus Christ is the fulfillment of these prophecies, offering himself as the sacrificial lamb to redeem humanity from sin (Hahn, 2009). This act of ultimate sacrifice institutes a new covenant, encapsulated in the sacraments of the Catholic Church, thus providing a theological basis for the transition from Judaism to Catholicism.

Moreover, the understanding of salvation in Catholicism is deeply seated in the person of Jesus Christ and his resurrection. This belief transcends the expectations of a temporal messianic kingdom and propounds an eternal salvation, accessible to all who believe in him and partake in the sacraments instituted by him. Such a conceptualization of salvation magnifies the universal scope of Jesus' mission, where the barriers between Jews and Gentiles are broken, inviting all into the family of God (Bruce, 2014).

The sacraments, particularly Baptism, Confirmation, and the Eucharist, are viewed as the new means of God's covenantal grace. They are not just symbolic rituals but are believed to be actual encounters with Christ and channels of grace. Through Baptism, one is spiritually reborn, shedding the original sin and becoming a new creation in Christ, which mirrors the Jewish ritual of Mikvah but fulfills it by imparting sanctifying grace. The sacrament of Confirmation strengthens this newfound faith, bestowing upon the believer the gifts of the Holy Spirit, reminiscent of the divine empowerment prophesied in Jewish scriptures. The Eucharist, or the Holy Communion, is the pinnacle of Christian life, offering the believers a share in the body and blood of Christ, as a perpetual Passover Lamb, ensuring their spiritual sustenance (Boersma, 2017).

This transition from old to new covenant is not a rejection of Jewish faith but rather its consummation. It acknowledges the enduring value of the Jewish covenant while presenting the new covenant through Jesus Christ as the completion of God's salvific plan. The Church Fathers have seen this transition as a fulfillment of the law and prophets, where the moral and ceremonial laws find their ultimate purpose in the teachings and person of Christ. Thus, embracing Catholicism as a Jew is seen not as conversion to a foreign faith but as completing one's journey towards salvation as foretold by the prophets.

The concept of the Church as the new Israel further elucidates this theological justification. Just as Israel was chosen to be the people through whom God would reveal His laws, the Catholic Church is considered the new vessel through which the grace of God is dispensed to the world. This ecclesiological perspective does not supplant the Jewish people but extends the divine promise to a universal audience, redefining the chosen people as all who would believe in Jesus Christ and adhere to His teachings.

The role of Mary, the mother of Jesus, also embodies a significant theological bridge between Judaism and Catholicism. Honored as the new Eve, her obedience and faith counterbalance the disobedience of Eve in the Genesis narrative. Mary's role in salvation history is thus seen as a pivotal junction that further fulfills Jewish expectations of the woman prophesied in Genesis who would play a crucial role in the battle against sin. Her perpetual virginity and motherhood offer a profound typology that resonates with the Jewish understanding of holiness and purity.

In the continuity of the priesthood, Catholicism sees the fulfillment of the Jewish priesthood. The sacramental priesthood instituted by Christ at the Last Supper, where he commands his disciples to do in memory of him what he had done, signifies the transition from the Levitical priesthood to the New Covenant priesthood. This change does not abrogate the promises made to Aaron and his descendants but elevates the priesthood to a universal level, making it an eternal mediator between God and humanity through Jesus Christ, the High Priest.

The celebration of the Lord's Day, Sunday, as the primary day of worship in Catholicism, also ties into Jewish tradition. It marks the new creation inaugurated by the resurrection of Jesus, just as the Sabbath celebrated God's creation of the world. This shift from Sabbath to Sunday worship is not a departure from Jewish tradition but a continuation of the biblical theme of creation and recreation, celebrating the fulfillment of messianic promises.

Catholicism's view of scripture further bridges Judaism and Catholic faith. The Catholic Church venerates the Hebrew Scriptures as an integral part of its Bible, recognizing the Old Testament as the word of God and essential for understanding the New Testament. The Church sees the Old Testament as preparatory to the coming of Christ, who is believed to be present in these ancient texts in the form of prophecy and typology. This reverence for the Hebrew Scriptures demonstrates the continuity of divine revelation, culminating in the person of Jesus Christ.

The principle of Sola Scriptura, while not a Catholic doctrine, finds its fulfillment in the Catholic teaching that the Bible cannot be understood apart from the tradition and teaching authority of the Church. This notion resonates with the Jewish understanding of the Oral Torah as necessary for interpreting the Written Torah. The Catholic Church's Magisterium serves a similar function, providing a living interpretative authority that ensures the fidelity of Christian doctrine to apostolic teaching.

Theological reflection on suffering and redemption further connects Jewish and Catholic spirituality. The notion of messianic suffering, evident in the suffering servant songs of Isaiah, finds its culmination in the passion and death of Jesus Christ. The Catholic understanding of redemptive suffering not only echoes the Jewish concept of suffering but elevates it to a means of participating in Christ's own redemptive work, offering a profound explanation for the role of suffering in the life of believers.

In conclusion, the theological justification for converting from Judaism to Catholicism is deeply rooted in the scriptures, traditions, and teachings that highlight the fulfillment of the Jewish faith in Christ. The transition to Catholicism is not seen as abandonment but as a fulfillment of the spiritual journey begun with the covenant between God and Abraham. It invites believers into a deeper understanding of salvation history, where the promises of old find their completion in the new covenant established by Jesus Christ.

The Feast of Faith: Embracing Catholic Truth

In the journey that traverses from the ancient traditions of Judaism to the profound depths of Catholicism, one discovers a road paved with the richness of shared heritage, theological fulfillment, and divine promise. The completion of this pilgrimage, encapsulated within the heart of Catholic faith, stands not as a departure from Jewish roots but as their full blossoming. Thus, the Feast of Faith is laid before us, inviting all to partake in the richness of Catholic truth.

The sacraments of Initiation - Baptism, Confirmation, and the Eucharist - serve not merely as rituals but as profound passages that usher the faithful into a more intimate communion with the Divine. In the context of our shared Abrahamic lineage, these sacraments are seen not as replacements but as the fulfillment of the Jewish agricultural feasts. Each step, from Baptism's cleansing waters to the Eucharist's communal wine, beckons us closer to the heart of divine revelation.

As we have explored, the transformation from barley to wheat in the believer's journey mirrors the spiritual evolution from Judaism to Catholicism. This progression is neither an abandonment of roots nor a disregard of heritage. Rather, it is a continuation, a growth that respects and fulfills the ancient promises delivered to our forefathers.

The Catholic Church, in its wisdom and through the ages, has meticulously preserved the essence of these ancient truths, manifesting them in the sacraments that guide one towards salvation. These divine instruments of grace are not merely symbolic but are active and living channels that effectuate the deepest communion with God.

Addressing and welcoming Jewish believers into the fold of Catholicism involves a respectful and loving engagement, recognizing the common ground we share and the profound fulfillment Catholicism offers to the Jewish expectation of Messianic salvation. It is a journey of discovery, open to all who seek the face of God with a sincere heart.

The Feast of Faith, therefore, calls out not just to those of Jewish heritage but to all seekers of truth. It offers the bread of life and the cup of eternal salvation to anyone willing to step into the embrace of Catholic tradition. Herein lies an open invitation: to taste and see that the Lord is good, to partake in the feast that eternally satisfies the soul.

This engagement with divine truth does not eschew scientific inquiry or dismiss rigorous academic study. On the contrary, the Catholic faith embraces reason and faith as complementary, encouraging a deeper exploration of our world and the mysteries of divine revelation. The Church stands as a beacon of both faith and reason, guiding the faithful through the complexities of modern life and the timeless questions of existence.

Through the lens of Catholic theology, every aspect of creation reveals a facet of divine wisdom and love. The sacraments, as outward signs instituted by Christ, provide a tangible means through which we participate in this divine mystery. They mark key moments in the journey of faith, grounding us in the reality of God's grace at work in our lives.

The Feast of Faith thus transcends temporal celebrations, offering an eternal banquet wherein the soul is nourished and prepared for its ultimate union with the Divine. It is in this feast that the full meaning of conversion and salvation is found—a conversion that is continuous, inviting us to grow deeper in love and closer to God.

As we conclude this exploration of the Feast of Faith, let us reflect on the beauty and depth of the Catholic truth. It is a truth that invites exploration, challenges preconceptions, and calls for a personal encounter with the living God. It is in this encounter that we find not just answers but meaning, not just salvation but a call to sanctity.

In embracing Catholic truth, we find ourselves part of a historical continuum, connected to the sacred tradition that spans millennia. This tradition, enriched by the wisdom of the Church Fathers and the sanctity of the saints, offers a path to profound spiritual fulfillment and eternal happiness.

The Feast of Faith, therefore, is more than a culmination; it is an ongoing invitation. It beckons every soul towards the glorious banquet prepared by God Himself. Here, at the feast, we find not only the fulfillment of Jewish prophecy and tradition but the universal call to holiness that resonates with every human heart.

Let us, therefore, approach this feast with hearts open to receive, minds eager to understand, and souls prepared to embrace the boundless love and mercy of God. For in the Feast of Faith, we truly encounter the essence of Catholic truth—a truth that satisfies the deepest longings of the human heart and offers the promise of eternal life.

In closing, may this journey through the fields of faith encourage and inspire all who seek to deepen their understanding of and relationship with the Divine. May the Feast of Faith be a source of strength, a beacon of hope, and a wellspring of inspiration, guiding all towards the embrace of Catholic truth and the joy of eternal communion with God.

References:

Glossary of Terms

In the progression toward a deeper understanding and appreciation of the Holy Roman Catholic Church and its theological, liturgical, and scriptural underpinnings, particularly as they relate to and fulfill Judaism, a well-defined glossary becomes an indispensable tool. Within these terms, one discovers not only definitions but also the spiritual bridges connecting ancient Judaic practices to their fulfillment in Catholicism. Herein, we elucidate a selection of terms pivotal to grasping the essence of both traditions and their interconnections.

Agricultural Feasts

Refers to the Jewish festivals, namely Passover, Pentecost, and Tabernacles, rooted in agricultural cycles and marked by thanksgiving for God's providence. These feasts symbolize spiritual truths within Catholicism, where they find a deeper, fulfilled meaning through Jesus Christ and the establishment of new sacraments.

Baptism

In Catholicism, Baptism acts as the initiatory sacrament of faith and entry into the Christian life (Catechism of the Catholic Church [CCC], 1993). Mirroring the Jewish practice of ritual washing, Baptism signifies purification and a new beginning in the body of Christ.

Confirmation

This sacrament strengthens and deepens the grace received at Baptism, marking the confirmed believer with a greater outpouring of the Holy Spirit (CCC, 1993). It echoes the Jewish feast of Pentecost, where the Holy Spirit descended upon the apostles, empowering them.

Eucharist

The Eucharist, or Holy Communion, is the source and summit of the Catholic faith, where believers partake of the Body and Blood of Christ (CCC, 1993). This sacrament fulfills the Jewish Passover with its sacrificial lamb, now replaced by Jesus' sacrifice, offering eternal salvation.

Jewish Converts to Catholicism

Individuals of Jewish heritage who embrace the Catholic faith, recognizing it as the fulfillment of the promises made to Israel and the expansion of God's covenant through Jesus Christ.

Theological Justification

The foundational rationale, drawn from Scripture and Tradition, for the transition from the Old Covenant established with the Jewish people to the New Covenant in Jesus Christ. This elucidates how Catholicism serves as the continuation and fulfillment of Judaism.

Sacramental Theology

A branch of theology that explores the nature, purpose, and effects of the sacraments. It asserts that sacraments are efficacious signs of grace, instituted by Christ and entrusted to the Church, through which divine life is dispensed to believers (CCC, 1993).

Through these terms, the reader gains insight into the rich tapestry of beliefs and practices that bind the heritage of Judaism with the fulfillment found in Catholicism. This glossary serves not merely as a repository of definitions but as a beacon guiding the faithful toward a profound comprehension of their faith's roots and its divine trajectory towards salvation.

Appendix A: Comparative Timeline of Jewish Feasts and Catholic Sacraments

The journey from the Jewish faith to Catholicism is both profound and deeply intricate, embodying a transition that spans not only theological but also temporal realms. This appendix endeavors to elucidate the comparative timeline of Jewish Feasts and Catholic Sacraments, drawing parallels that reveal the inherent continuity between these two great traditions. Such an exploration intends to establish Catholicism as not merely a successor but as a fulfillment of Judaism, highlighting the means by which salvation is proffered to humanity through the Church.

Jewish Passover and Catholic Baptism: The Initiation Rites

The Passover, significant in Judaism for celebrating the Israelites' liberation from Egyptian bondage, correspondingly echoes the theme of liberation in Catholicism through the sacrament of Baptism. Just as the Passover marked the beginning of a journey towards the Promised Land, Baptism represents the Christian's initiation into a life of faith, cleansing them from original sin and commencing their spiritual journey towards the heavenly promise. This parallel not only signifies a continuation but deepens the understanding of spiritual emancipation and renewal.

Shavuot (Pentecost) and Confirmation: Empowerment by the Spirit

The festival of Shavuot, or Pentecost as it is known in Christianity, celebrates the giving of the Torah to the Israelites and, similarly, the descent of the Holy Spirit upon the apostles. The Jewish feast commemorates divine revelation and the cementing of the covenant, while the Catholic sacrament of Confirmation strengthens the bond between the believer and the Church, enriched by the gifts of the Holy Spirit. This shared emphasis on spiritual empowerment and commitment underscores the unified trajectory from Jewish tradition to Catholic fulfillment.

Sukkot (Tabernacles) and The Eucharist: Union with the Divine

Sukkot, or the Feast of Tabernacles, wherein the Israelites lived in temporary shelters to recall their dependence on God during their desert wanderings, finds its Catholic counterpart in the Sacrament of the Eucharist. This sacrament, central to Catholic faith, is the true Communion with Christ, embodying the believer's union with the Divine. Just as Sukkot celebrates God's provision and presence with Israel, the Eucharist celebrates Christ's sacrifice and continual presence in His Church, offering the nourishment of His Body and Blood.

Comparative Significance and Theological Continuity

The aforementioned parallels form the cornerstone of a broader theological and spiritual continuity between Judaism and Catholicism. The sequence from Passover through Shavot to Sukkot mirrors the Christian theological journey from liberation in Baptism, empowerment in Confirmation, to union in the Eucharist. This comparative timeline isn't merely about drawing parallels for the sake of comparison; it's about understanding the salvific plan of God that culminates in the fullness of revelation in Jesus Christ and His Church.

Through this exploration, it becomes evident that the Catholic Sacraments are not a repudiation but rather a continuation and fulfillment of the Jewish feasts. Each step in this journey reveals God's consistent invitation to humanity for a deeper communion and revelation. The Church's sacraments, seen in this light, extend the ancient paths of Jewish faith, leading believers to the fulfillment of God's promises through Jesus Christ.

As we ponder on these sacred traditions, it is crucial for both Jewish believers transitioning into Catholicism and Catholics seeking to deepen their faith to appreciate the rich tapestry of salvation history. The Church, in its wisdom, has always sought to honor its Judaic roots while proclaiming the inexhaustible richness of Christ's salvation, a testament to the Church's role as the means of salvation for all, Jews and Gentiles alike.

In sum, the comparative exploration of Jewish Feasts and Catholic Sacraments as outlined in this appendix serves to affirm the Catholic Church not only as the custodian of divine grace through the Sacraments but also as the fulfillment of the spiritual journey delineated in Jewish tradition. It's a journey that has always been oriented towards salvation, a journey that finds its completion in the embrace of Catholic truth.

Appendix B: Resources for Further Study

In pursuit of a deeper understanding and appreciation of the journey from Judaism to Catholicism, one must engage with a broad spectrum of resources that enrich knowledge and foster spiritual growth. This appendix is dedicated to offering a curated list of academic, biblical, and scientific resources that serve as a foundation for further exploration into the rich traditions and theological connections between Judaism and Catholicism. The goal is to provide students, university professors, biblical scholars, and converts with a compilation of materials that will aid in the exaltation and propagation of the Holy Roman Catholic Church, the conversion process, and the establishment of Catholicism as the fulfillment and means of salvation that Judaism anticipates.

For a succinct yet profound overview of the historical roots connecting Jewish agricultural feasts to Catholic sacraments, the academic works by scholars such as Cohen et al. (2019) provide a solid starting point. Their research illuminates the symbolic and theological bridges between ancient Jewish practices and Christian sacraments, offering a rich tapestry of insights for those intrigued by the spiritual significance of barley, wheat, and grapes in scriptural traditions.

Understanding the sacraments of initiation in Catholicism, which are baptism, confirmation, and the Eucharist, requires delving into the works of early Church Fathers as well as contemporary Catholic theologians. Exploring the depths of these sacraments and their roots in Jewish customs can be significantly enhanced by engaging with the seminal texts by figures such as Augustine and Aquinas, alongside modern interpretations by theologians like Ratzinger (2007), ensuring a balance between historical theology and contemporary understanding.

As converts and believers seek a deeper connection between Passover and baptism, Pentecost and confirmation, and Tabernacles and the Eucharist, they are encouraged to explore scriptural exegesis from both Jewish and Catholic perspectives. This involves a concerted study of key biblical texts, aided by commentaries that elucidate the agricultural metaphors and their spiritual implications within both faith traditions (Boersma, 2017).

To further explore the transformation within believers, as discussed in the journey from barley to wheat, and the theological justification for seeing Catholicism as the continuation of Judaism, scholarly articles and books that examine conversion narratives provide invaluable insights. These resources reveal the personal and communal aspects of faith transitions, underlining the promise of salvation that underpins the Catholic Church's appeal to Jewish individuals (Levy, 1924).

For those particularly interested in sacramental theology and the role of sacraments in salvation, an in-depth study of Catholic doctrine is crucial. The Catechism of the Catholic Church stands as a primary resource in this regard, complemented by theological analyses that explore the nuances of grace, divinity, and redemption through the sacraments. Works by theologians such as Von Balthasar (2018) offer profound insights into the mystery and beauty of Catholic sacraments, drawing connections to their Jewish roots and wider scriptural narratives.

Addressing common objections and misunderstandings between Jewish and Catholic beliefs necessitates an approach rooted in dialogue and mutual respect. Engaging with interdisciplinary studies that incorporate biblical scholarship, history, and theology, such as those by Goldman et al. (2022), helps in articulating informed and compassionate responses to theological queries, fostering an environment where faith traditions can be explored and understood in depth.

The commitment to converting hearts and minds to the Catholic faith, while recognizing the rich spiritual heritage of Judaism, is a journey that benefits greatly from a careful study of missionary strategies, interfaith dialogues, and conversion testimonies. Resources that compile these experiences, alongside theological reflections on the process of conversion, serve as a guide for those involved in the spiritual guidance of Jewish converts to Catholicism.

In conclusion, the wealth of resources available for further study offers a comprehensive framework for understanding the intricate relationship between Judaism and Catholicism. It is through academic scholarship, biblical study, and scientific inquiry that the fullness of faith is revealed, guiding individuals and communities towards a deeper appreciation of the sacramental and salvific journey from Jewish heritage to Catholic belief.

References

1. Catechism of the Catholic Church. (1994). Vatican City: Libreria Editrice Vaticana.

2. Hahn, S. (2009). The Lamb's Supper: The Mass as Heaven on Earth. Doubleday Religion.

3. Pitre, B. (2011). Jesus and the Jewish Roots of the Eucharist: Unlocking the Secrets of the Last Supper. Doubleday.

4. Logic, S. (2020). Wheat and Chaff: Decoding the Meaning of the Biblical Proverbs. Secret Bible Knowledge and Lost Wisdom. (n.p.): Independently Published.

5. 1 Corinthians 5:7. The New American Bible, Revised Edition. (2011). Washington, DC: The United States Conference of Catholic Bishops.

6. 2 Corinthians 5:17

7. Bruce, D. (2014). He Is the One: Proof from the Hebrew Scriptures That Jesus Was the Jewish Messiah. (n.p.): CreateSpace Independent Publishing Platform.

8.   Leviticus. (n.d.). The Holy Bible.

9.   The Book of Ruth

10.   The Catechism of the Catholic Church. (1994). Vatican: Libreria Editrice Vaticana.

11.   Benedict XVI. (2007). Sacramentum Caritatis. Libreria Editrice Vaticana.

12.   Catechism of the Catholic Church (CCC). (1999). 2nd ed. Vatican: Libreria Editrice Vaticana.

13.   Catechism of the Catholic Church. (1992). 2nd ed., Vatican: Libreria Editrice Vaticana..

14.   Catechism of the Catholic Church. (1992). Vatican: Libreria Editrice Vaticana.

15.   Catechism of the Catholic Church. (1993). 2nd Ed. Vatican: Libreria Editrice Vaticana.

16.   Catechism of the Catholic Church. (1994). 2nd Ed. Washington, DC: United States Catholic Conference..

17.   Congar, Y. (1966). Tradition and Traditions: An Historical and a Theological Essay. Macmillan.

18. Congar, Y. (2010). The Mystery of the Church. London: Geoffrey Chapman.

19. Dei Verbum. (1965). Dogmatic Constitution on Divine Revelation. Vatican Council II. Vatican City: Vatican Press.

20. Exodus 12:1-14

21. Exodus 12:1-28.

22. Hahn, S. (2005). The Lamb's Supper: The Mass as Heaven on Earth. Darton, Longman & Todd.

23. Hahn, S. (2010). The Lamb's Supper: The Mass as Heaven on Earth. New York: Image Books.

24. Heschel, A. J. (1955). God in search of man: A philosophy of Judaism. New York: Farrar, Straus and Giroux.

25. Holy Bible. New Revised Standard Version.

26. John 3:5

27. John 7:37-39; 15:1.

28. John Paul II. Christifideles Laici. Libreria Editrice Vaticana, 1988.

29. Levy, R. M. (1924). Why Jews Become Catholics: Authentic Narratives. United States: author.

30. Lumen Gentium. (1964). Dogmatic Constitution on the Church. Second Vatican Council.

31. Neusner, J. (1993). Judaism when Christianity Began: A Survey of Belief and Practice. Louisville, KY: Westminster John Knox Press.

32. Neusner, J. (1994). Judaism when Christianity began: A survey of belief and practice. Louisville: Westminster John Knox Press.

33. Neusner, J., Avery-Peck, A.J., & Green, W.S. (Eds.). (2001). The Encyclopaedia of Judaism. Brill.

34. New American Bible. (1970). Confraternity of Christian Doctrine.

35. Ratzinger, J. (2007). Jesus of Nazareth. New York, NY: Doubleday.

36. Ratzinger, J. (2007). Introduction to Christianity. Ignatius Press.

37. Scott, B. (1997). The Feasts of Israel: Seasons of the Messiah. United States: Friends of Israel Gospel Ministry.

38. Boersma, H. (2017). Scripture as Real Presence: Sacramental Exegesis in the Early Church. United States: Baker Publishing Group.

39. Acts 2:1-4

40. Romans 6:3-4

41. Vatican II. (1965). Nostra aetate: Declaration on the Relation of the Church to Non-Christian Religions. Vatican: Vatican Press.

42. Von Balthasar, H. (2018). The role of the sacraments in the divine plan of salvation. Theological Studies Press.

THE 15 PRAYERS OF ST. BRIDGET

 These Prayers and these Promises have been copied from a book printed in Toulouse in 1740 and published by the P. Adrien Parvilliers of the Company of Jesus, Apostolic Missionary of the Holy Land, with approbation, permission and recommendation to distribute them.
Pope Pius IX took cognisance of these Prayers with the prologue; he approved them May 31, 1862, recognising them as true and for the good of souls.

As St. Bridget for a long time wanted to know the number of blows Our Lord received during His Passion, He one day appeared to her and said: "I received 5480 blows on My Body. If you wish to honour them in some way, say 15 Our Fathers and 15 Hail Marys with the following Prayers (which He taught her) for a whole year. When the year is up, you will have honoured each one of My Wounds."

He made the following promises to anyone who recited these Prayers for a whole year:

1. I will deliver 15 souls of his lineage from Purgatory.

2. 15 souls of his lineage will be confirmed and preserved in grace.

3. 15 sinners of his lineage will be converted.

4. Whoever recites these Prayers will attain the first degree of perfection.

5. 15 days before his death I will give him My Precious Body in order that he may escape eternal starvation;

I will give him My Precious Blood to drink lest he thirst eternally.

6. 15 days before his death he will feel a deep contrition for all his sins and will have a perfect knowledge of them.

7. I will place before him the sign of My Victorious Cross for his help and defence against the attacks of his enemies.

8. Before his death I shall come with My Dearest Beloved Mother.

9. I shall graciously receive his soul, and will lead it into eternal joys.

10. And having led it there I shall give him a special draught from the fountain of My Deity, something I will not for those who have not recited My Prayers.

11. Let it be known that whoever may have been living in a state of mortal sin for 30 years, but who will recite devoutly, or have the intention to recite these Prayers, the Lord will forgive him all his sins.

12. I shall protect him from strong temptations.

13. I shall preserve and guard his 5 senses.

14. I shall preserve him from a sudden death.

15. His soul will be delivered from eternal death.

16. He will obtain all he asks for from God and the Blessed Virgin.

17. If he has lived all his life doing his own will and he is to die the next day, his life will be prolonged.

18. Every time one recites these Prayers he gains 100 days indulgence.

19. He is assured of being joined to the supreme Choir of Angels.

20. Whoever teaches these Prayers to another, will have continuous joy and merit which will endure eternally.

21. There where these Prayers are being said or will be said in the future God is present with His grace.

Each prayer is preceded by one Our Father and one Hail Mary.

Our Father, who art in heaven, hallowed be thy name.
Thy kingdom come.
Thy will be done on earth as it is in heaven.
Give us this day our daily bread and forgive us our
trespasses as we forgive those who trespass against us and
lead us not into temptation but deliver us from evil. **Amen**

Hail Mary, full of grace, the Lord is with thee; blessed art
thou among women and blessed is the fruit of thy womb,
Jesus.
Holy Mary, Mother of God, pray for us sinners, now and at
the hour of our death. **Amen.**

FIRST PRAYER
Our Father – Hail Mary.
O Jesus Christ! Eternal Sweetness to those who love Thee,
joy surpassing all joy and all desire, Salvation and Hope of
all sinners, Who hast proved that Thou hast no greater
desire than to be among men, even assuming human nature

at the fullness of time for the love of men, recall all the sufferings Thou hast endured from the instant of Thy conception, and especially during Thy Passion, as it was decreed and ordained from all eternity in the Divine plan.

Remember, O Lord, that during the Last Supper with Thy disciples, having washed their feet, Thou gavest them Thy Most Precious Body and Blood, and while at the same time thou didst sweetly console them, Thou didst foretell them Thy coming Passion.
Remember the sadness and bitterness which Thou didst experience in Thy Soul as Thou Thyself bore witness saying: "My Soul is sorrowful even unto death."

Remember all the fear, anguish and pain that Thou didst suffer in Thy delicate Body before the torment of the Crucifixion, when, after having prayed three times, bathed in a sweat of blood, Thou wast betrayed by Judas, Thy disciple, arrested by the people of a nation Thou hadst chosen and elevated, accused by false witnesses, unjustly judged by three judges during the flower of Thy youth and during the solemn Paschal season.

Remember that Thou wast despoiled of Thy garments and clothed in those of derision; that Thy Face and Eyes were veiled, that Thou wast buffeted, crowned with thorns, a reed placed in Thy Hands, that Thou was crushed with blows and overwhelmed with affronts and outrages.
In memory of all these pains and sufferings which Thou didst endure before Thy Passion on the Cross, grant me before my death true contrition, a sincere and entire confession, worthy satisfaction and the remission of all my sins. **Amen.**

SECOND PRAYER
Our Father – Hail Mary.
O Jesus! True liberty of angels, Paradise of delights, remember the horror and sadness which Thou didst endure

when Thy enemies, like furious lions, surrounded Thee, and by thousands of insults, spits, blows, lacerations and other unheard-of-cruelties, tormented Thee at will.

In consideration of these torments and insulting words, I beseech Thee, O my Saviour, to deliver me from all my enemies, visible and invisible, and to bring me, under Thy protection, to the perfection of eternal salvation. **Amen.**

THIRD PRAYER
Our Father – Hail Mary.
O Jesus! Creator of Heaven and earth Whom nothing can encompass or limit, Thou Who dost enfold and hold all under Thy Loving power, remember the very bitter pain.

Thou didst suffer when the Jews nailed Thy Sacred Hands and Feet to the Cross by blow after blow with big blunt nails, and not finding Thee in a pitiable enough state to satisfy their rage, they enlarged Thy Wounds, and added pain to pain, and with indescribable cruelty stretched Thy Body on the Cross, pulled Thee from all sides, thus dislocating Thy Limbs.

I beg of Thee, O Jesus, by the memory of this most Loving suffering of the Cross, to grant me the grace to fear Thee and to Love Thee. **Amen.**

FOURTH PRAYER
Our Father – Hail Mary.
O Jesus! Heavenly Physician, raised aloft on the Cross to heal our wounds with Thine, remember the bruises which Thou didst suffer and the weakness of all Thy Members which were distended to such a degree that never was there pain like unto Thine.

From the crown of Thy Head to the Soles of Thy Feet there

was not one spot on Thy Body that was not in torment, and yet, forgetting all Thy sufferings, Thou didst not cease to pray to Thy Heavenly Father for Thy enemies, saying: "Father forgive them for they know not what they do."

Through this great Mercy, and in memory of this suffering, grant that the remembrance of Thy Most Bitter Passion may effect in us a perfect contrition and the remission of all our sins. **Amen**.

FIFTH PRAYER
Our Father – Hail Mary.
O Jesus! Mirror of eternal splendour, remember the sadness which Thou experienced, when contemplating in the light of Thy Divinity the predestination of those who would be saved by the merits of Thy Sacred Passion.

Thou didst see at the same time, the great multitude of reprobates who would be damned for their sins, and Thou didst complain bitterly of those hopeless lost and unfortunate sinners.

Through this abyss of compassion and pity, and especially through the goodness which Thou displayed to the good thief when Thou saidst to him: "This day, thou shalt be with Me in Paradise." I beg of Thee, O Sweet Jesus, that at the hour of my death, Thou wilt show me mercy. **Amen**.

SIXTH PRAYER
Our Father – Hail Mary.
O Jesus! Beloved and most desirable King, remember the grief Thou didst suffer, when naked and like a common criminal.

Thou was fastened and raised on the Cross, when all Thy relatives and friends abandoned Thee, except Thy Beloved

Mother, who remained close to Thee during Thy agony and whom Thou didst entrust to Thy faithful disciple when Thou saidst to Mary: "Woman, behold thy son!" and to St. John: "Son, behold thy Mother!"

I beg of Thee O my Saviour, by the sword of sorrow which pierced the soul of Thy holy Mother, to have compassion on me in all my affliction and tribulations, both corporal and spiritual, and to assist me in all my trials, and especially at the hour of my death. **Amen**.

SEVENTH PRAYER
Our Father – Hail Mary.
O Jesus! Inexhaustible Fountain of compassion, Who by a profound gesture of Love, said from the Cross: "I thirst!" suffered from the thirst for the salvation of the human race.

I beg of Thee O my Saviour, to inflame in our hearts the desire to tend toward perfection in all our acts; and to extinguish in us the concupiscence of the flesh and the ardor of worldly desires. **Amen**.

EIGHTH PRAYER
Our Father – Hail Mary.
O Jesus! Sweetness of hearts, delight of the spirit, by the bitterness of the vinegar and gall which Thou didst taste on the Cross for Love of us, grant us the grace to receive worthily.

Thy Precious Body and Blood during our life and at the hour of our death, that they may serve as a remedy and consolation for our souls. **Amen.**

NINTH PRAYER
Our Father – Hail Mary.

O Jesus! Royal virtue, joy of the mind, recall the pain Thou
didst endure when, plunged in an ocean of bitterness at the
approach of death, insulted, outraged by the Jews.

Thou didst cry out in a loud voice that Thou was abandoned
by Thy Father, saying: "My God, My God, why hast Thou
forsaken me?"

Through this anguish, I beg of Thee, O my Saviour, not to
abandon me in the terrors and pains of my death. **Amen.**

TENTH PRAYER
Our Father – Hail Mary.
O Jesus! Who art the beginning and end of all things, life and
virtue, remembers that for our sakes Thou was plunged in
an abyss of suffering from the soles of Thy Feet to the crown
of Thy Head.

In consideration of the enormity of Thy Wounds, teach me to
keep, through pure love, Thy Commandments, whose way is
wide and easy for those who love Thee. **Amen.**

ELEVENTH PRAYER
Our Father – Hail Mary.
O Jesus! Deep abyss of mercy, I beg of Thee, in memory of
Thy Wounds which penetrated to the very marrow of Thy
Bones and to the depth of Thy being, to draw me, a
miserable sinner, overwhelmed by my offenses, away from
sin and to hide me from Thy Face justly irritated against me,
hide me in Thy wounds, until Thy anger and just indignation
shall have passed away. **Amen.**

TWELFTH PRAYER
Our Father – Hail Mary.
O Jesus! Mirror of Truth, symbol of unity, bond of charity,

remember the multitude of wounds with which Thou wast afflicted from head to foot, torn and reddened by the spilling of Thy adorable Blood. O great and universal pain, which Thou didst suffer in Thy virginal flesh for love of us! Sweetest Jesus! What is there that Thou couldst have done for us which Thou has not done!

May the fruit of Thy suffering be renewed in my soul by the faithful remembrance of Thy Passion, and may Thy love increase in my heart each day, until I see Thee in eternity: Thou Who art the treasure of every real good and every joy, which I beg Thee to grant me, O Sweetest Jesus, in heaven. **Amen.**

THIRTEENTH PRAYER
Our Father – Hail Mary.
O Jesus! Strong Lion, Immortal and Invincible King, remember the pain which Thou didst endure when all Thy strength, both moral and physical, was entirely exhausted, Thou didst bow Thy Head, saying: "It is consummated!"

Through this anguish and grief, I beg of Thee Lord Jesus, to have mercy on me at the hour of my death when my mind will be greatly troubled and my soul will be in anguish. **Amen.**

FOURTEENTH PRAYER
Our Father – Hail Mary.
O Jesus! Only Son of the Father, Splendour and Figure of His Substance, remember the simple and humble recommendation.

Thou didst make of Thy Soul to Thy Eternal Father, saying: "Father, into Thy Hands I commend My Spirit!" And with Thy Body all torn, and Thy Heart Broken, and the bowels of Thy Mercy open to redeem us, Thou didst Expire.

By this Precious Death, I beg of Thee O King of Saints, comfort me and help me to resist the devil, the flesh and the world, so that being dead to the world I may live for Thee alone.

I beg of Thee at the hour of my death to receive me, a pilgrim and an exile returning to Thee. **Amen.**

FIFTEENTH PRAYER
Our Father – Hail Mary.
O Jesus! True and fruitful Vine! Remember the abundant outpouring of Blood which Thou didst so generously shed from Thy Sacred Body as juice from grapes in a wine press.

From Thy Side, pierced with a lance by a soldier, blood and water issued forth until there was not left in Thy Body a single drop, and finally, like a bundle of myrrh lifted to the top of the Cross Thy delicate Flesh was destroyed, the very Substance of Thy Body withered, and the Marrow of Thy Bones dried up.

Through this bitter Passion and through the outpouring of Thy Precious Blood, I beg of Thee, O Sweet Jesus, to receive my soul when I am in my death agony. **Amen.**

CONCLUSION
O Sweet Jesus! Pierce my heart so that my tears of penitence and love will be my bread day and night; may I be converted entirely to Thee, may my heart be Thy perpetual habitation, may my conversation be pleasing to Thee, and may the end of my life be so praiseworthy that I may merit Heaven and there with Thy saints, praise Thee
forever. **Amen.**